Tangled Up in
Red, White, and Blue

Tangled Up in Red, White, and Blue

New Social Movements in America

Christine A. Kelly

ROWMAN & LITTLEFIELD PUBLISHERS, INC.
Lanham • Boulder • New York • Oxford

ROWMAN & LITTLEFIELD PUBLISHERS, INC.

Published in the United States of America
by Rowman & Littlefield Publishers, Inc.
4720 Boston Way, Lanham, Maryland 20706
http://www.rowmanlittlefield.com

12 Hid's Copse Road
Cumnor Hill, Oxford OX2 9JJ, England

British Library Cataloguing in Publication Information Available

Library of Congress Cataloging-in-Publication Data
Kelly, Christine A., 1961–
    Tangled up in red, white, and blue : new social movements in America / Christine A. Kelly.
        p. cm.
    Includes bibliographical references and index.
    ISBN 0-7425-0812-9 (cloth : alk. paper)—ISBN 0-7425-0813-7 (pbk. : alk. paper)
        1. Social movements—United States. 2. Ideology—United States. 3. Radicalism—United
States. 4. Pressure groups—United States. I. Title.

    HM881 .K45 2000
    303.48'4'0973—dc21

                                                                    00-057587

Printed in the United States of America

∞™ The paper used in this publication meets the minimum requirements of American
National Standard for Information Sciences—Permanence of Paper for Printed Library
Materials, ANSI/NISO Z39.48–1992.

This book is lovingly dedicated to my exceptional parents, Therese McKim Kelly and the late Thomas A. Kelly. Their nurturance, guidance, and ethics are the foundation of everything I do.

Contents

Preface

It is with surprising simplicity, I now realize, that this book took shape and finally emerged. That is not to say that it has been a simple process but only that as an act of scholarship, my academic work has never strayed far from my daily pursuits, concerns, and fundamentally political interests. The concerns raised in this book, I can honestly say, were forged from my own participation in several "new" social movements throughout my college and university years, as well as from the experience of rallies, protests, and organizing that punctuated my childhood and teenage years. For those of us who were born in the sixties, the events that rocked American culture—assassinations, sit-ins, rebellions, riots, war, felled heroes— and the names and places that exploded out of the white noise of ground shifting (Martin, Bobby, Malcolm, Angela, Nixon, Selma, Vietnam, Newark, Chicago, Kent State, Woodstock) became either a happily forgotten chapter or like a strange dream that you desperately try to remember upon waking. For me, as a child growing up in a liberal Catholic household devoted to a social gospel, the memories were concrete and both tragic and cherished.

In high school, I rode the crest of "No Nukes" concerts and marches and experienced firsthand the sense of purpose that comes from participating in a righteous cause. By 1983, however, when I enrolled at my state university, I felt alienated, isolated, and much at odds with the era, which seemed dominated by Reaganism and the drive for economic success. But then I began to discover the world of progressive student groups and meetings on campus. They were small, but they existed. And why not? Social change neither begins nor ends as abruptly as history books lead us to believe.

Between 1984 and 1992, I was lucky enough to experience and participate in the largest upsurge of student activism in the United States since the 1960s. I was a proud participant in the 1985 wave of anti-Apartheid protests that swept American campuses. I also belonged to a small feminist collective, organized numerous "CIA off-campus" campaigns, and participated in a considerable number of local, regional, national, and even international events and projects. While all of these experiences helped me conceptualize what social movements do, several key events (discussed in later chapters) provoked me to critically evaluate the dominant trends in social movement thinking and behavior. As the projects I was involved with became increasingly successful (i.e., engaging more and more campuses or groups in a broadening coalition or network), greater confusion about strategy, aims, and purposes also arose.

As the impulse toward consolidation of interests and resources developed among student groups, and the targets of protests switched from local authorities (like the University Board of Governors or a local dump site) to national and multinational authorities (such as the U.S. Department of Education, Exxon), students unraveled; they appeared ideologically confused, structurally inchoate, and seemingly unwilling (or unable) to assert a national or unified identity. Little of what we studied regarding the New Left, women's liberation, civil rights, or the counter culture helped us resolve this dilemma. The fantastic gains of the previous era, in terms of both culture and the law, seemed easily threatened by right-wing advances, especially in the absence of lasting counter institutions. Indeed, the seeming collapse of the New Left left indelible, albeit often unacknowledged, marks on our organizing styles and ideological rigging. As young activists, our search for continuity was tellingly marked by the seeking out of individuals—Abbie Hoffman, Al Haber, Mark Rudd, Angela Davis, Barbara Ehrenreich, Barbara Smith, Bobby Seale, and many others less well known. Our quest for guidance revealed as many different conclusions about the 1960s legacy as there were people on our lists. Ideologically, organizationally, and strategically there was no consensus among "the grown-ups." The disarray among the Left was, and continues to be, profound.

The sixties introduced a new kind politics to the American landscape that, in keeping with new social movement theorists' descriptions, was far less concerned with capturing state institutions. The noninstitutional trajectory, along with all the trappings of cultural politics, are inheritances that appeared increasingly troublesome in the eighties despite the gains of the sixties. The triumphs and the drama of the sixties seemed more like a shooting star than a legacy—shooting stars being, in reality, temporary streaks of lights that burn only once. In comparison, our presence, numbers, and energy seemed all but ignored. The ideological matrix upon which we operated did not yield significant national momentum or attention. Our own successes and the sense of control we experienced at the local level, compared with the utterly frustrating experience of regional and national organizing, led us to ask whether social movements were better off sticking with the local arena and conceding centers of power to those who already occupied that territory. In many respects, this same debate was responsible for the decline of significant student and youth organizing following the Gulf War and continues to haunt new social movements today.

Social movement life, as I experienced it between 1984 and 1992, allowed me to enjoy a previously unknown communal identity. Our collective dreams revealed fantastically ambitious intentions that involved endless debate, oddly construed collective strategies, exhilarating actions, conflict, exhaustion, and sometimes bitter feuding. All of this, in the midst of our drive for a more just society, presented overlapping dilemmas that begged the biggest question of all: How come we never seemed to get anywhere?

By the time I reached graduate school, I had come across the literature loosely referred to as "new social movement theory." Broadly speaking, this primarily European perspective focuses on the perception of increasingly centralizing global and structural developments which, it is argued, are simultaneously generating sociopolitical responses characterized by their antinomy to homogenizing forces. "New" social movements (NSMs), described as local, decentralized, and essentially progressive, are heralded as counterhegemonic institutions. This claim, to varying degrees, underlies the widely shared assumption that the decentralized form is controversial in and of itself. It is this claim in particular that I was inclined to doubt and thus is a recurring theme throughout this work. In light of concrete experience in NSMs of the type described in the literature, I questioned the prognosis while agreeing with many of the claims suggesting a link between systemic tendencies and new patterns of collective action. Here I discovered an intersection of my two emerging concerns: What characterizes the systemic context in which new social movements appear to arise? and What are the institutional limits and possibilities for new social movements in the American context? For me, sorting out the inconsistencies between systemic characterizations and actual movement outcomes required a closer look at the institutional and ideological variables between national contexts.

On several occasions, my participation in U.S. social movements led me into international settings (primarily European) where I was confronted with fundamentally different organizing cultures. Of course, there were many ideological counterparts: anarchists, greens, ecofeminists, socialists, and so on. Yet, the milieu, the ideological context, and the repertoires of actions seemed substantially broader, bolder, and more assured. In addition, European NSMs seemed, in a relative sense, more successful in terms of outcomes.[1] I considered whether the sweeping structural explanations offered in the literature, to the extent that they are valid, are mitigated by national institutional settings and ideological traditions. Maybe this could explain the gap between optimistic European NSM theorists and unhappy American activists. If so, what remained valid in the work of NSM theorists, and what was it, specifically, about the U.S. context, as compared with Europe, that proved less receptive to the impact of NSMs?

These questions form the basis of my inquiry here. While my answers are self-consciously experimental, I believe I have highlighted the fundamental need for social movement participants themselves to engage in serious efforts at self-understanding in relation to both systemic and contingent aspects of their contexts. Specifically, I hope to show that a critical understanding of the relationships between global economic trends, national institutions, and ideological possibilities can significantly aid contemporary progressive movements that struggle for a more reflexive movement ideology and greater impact. For those citizens concerned with the recovery and expansion of democratic norms and practice, theory must not be considered either a luxury or the province of academics. Practical imperatives now require a kind of social theory that is reflexive, speculative, and accessible. I can only hope that I have made a practical contribution toward that end here.

NOTE

1. Here the best example can be found in the Greens of Germany who, despite significant internal conflict and numerous setbacks, have found institutional expression while retaining radical roots in both feminist and environmental NSMs.

Acknowledgments

I am extremely grateful for all the help I have had putting this book together. Working with Rowman & Littlefield has been an altogether pleasant experience; special thanks go to my editor Steven Wrinn for his professionalism, good faith, and good cheer! I would also like to extend my gratitude to editorial assistant Mary Carpenter for keeping things on track and to production editor Dorothy Bradley.

While at Rutgers University, I had the opportunity to organize with some of the smartest, most generous, and most committed people around. In the 1980's, I was part of a unique local undergraduate community that managed to combine, in astounding ways, rigorous intellectual study and the ongoing grind of movement work (while holding down jobs.) During that time I was also lucky enough to strike up an apprentice relationship of sorts with U.S. dissident (as he liked to call himself) Abbie Hoffman. Aside from his difficulties with bipolar disorder, Mr. Hoffman was a magnanimous teacher whose ideas and organizing insights had, in my mind, only grown better with age. More important, he was passionately committed to "passing it on" and was one of the few figures of the 1960s who remained actively committed to youth politics. He was an honorable and keen teacher to anyone willing to keep pace with him. He deserves many thanks.

My formal education at Rutgers, both undergraduate and graduate, was peppered with great teachers and scholars, among them W. Carey McWilliams, Benjamin Barber, and Cynthia Daniels. I extend my deepest gratitude to Prof. Stephen Eric Bronner, not only for his role in encouraging my intellectual development, but also for the model he has provided for the thousands of students who have passed through his courses and seminars, with his combination of exacting standards, dedicated teaching, and progressive values. His intellectual influence on my work here is obvious. My wish is that it serves as a tribute to a great teacher; my shortcomings are, of course, my own. A special thanks to Frances Fox Piven for talking to me about my "topic" and generally enduring my pesky queries, and to another generous New Yorker, Barbara Handman of People for the American Way, for her mentorship and political tolerance.

I also received tremendous support while teaching at Mount Holyoke College (1996–1999). I want to thank the entire Department of Politics, especially Joan Cocks, Penny Gill, and Jean Grossholtz for their feedback and support, and administrative assistant Shirley Sudsbury for her helpfulness all along. In addition, I want to thank Dean Donal O'Shea and the Faculty Grants Committee for their generosity in awarding me support while I finished my revisions. As a result, I benefitted from the research assistance of three of Mount Holyoke's finest students: Amy Richardson, Amanda Ryan, and Renee Sweeney. An added thanks to all those wonderful women in my classes; I was challenged, invigorated, and altogether pleased with my fantastic students.

I also want to extend my thanks to Stan Luger and Dean Sandra Flake at the University of Northern Colorado for their support. Special thanks also go to Susan Craig, Manfred Steger, Elizabeth Kelly, Luis Eduardo Mendieta, Michael Forman, George Katsiafikas, John Eherenberg, Jennifer Frost, Rosalyn Baxandall, and Kathleen Casey for their various forms of assistance during this project. I owe much to Judith Grant for her comments on the entire manuscript as well. A warm thanks to Eliot Katz for his special assistance in the earliest stages. And to all my dearest friends: Gabrielle Wilders and Tony Shanahan, Jim Robinson and Sharon Baller, Lisa Adler and Don Kennell, Alane Poirier, Niamh Reilly, and Jenny Farquar for their unflinching support when I needed it most. And to those without whose help I might not have persevered—Nancy Azara, Linda Gonzalves, and Sandra Sup.

Lastly, profound gratitude to my wonderful family. I have been just plain lucky in this respect—thanks especially to my mother, Therese, whose confidence in me, and whose vision of the world, is nothing short of intoxicating; and to my dad who, unfortunately, passed away before I was able to complete this. He was a loving father, exemplary public servant, and committed citizen; among many other things, he gave me the itch for political science and writing. Thank you, Dad. I also want to thank my incredible siblings—all five of them—Daniel, Ritamarie, Maureen, Andrew, and Kathleen. I have never seen so much unconditional love in a family. You guys are the best! A warm thanks also to Gary Yudman. And to my beautiful son Dylan—thank you for being so patient while Mommy typed. You are my inspiration!

Finally, general thanks to Bob Dylan for etching his imagery onto the American imagination.

PART ONE

Theory and Social Movements

Introduction

This is a book about the role that progressive social movements might play in the recovery and expansion of democracy and justice in the new millennium. While positioned in the American context, this work is not merely concerned with the territory of the United States, but with any society in which the logic of markets and states overwhelms the democratic horizon. This is a book about the potential for the reclamation, reform, and enlightened transformation of the most expansive elements of the liberal tradition—that social and economic justice remain tangled in liberalism's web of pretentious institutions and betrayed promises is the reason for this battle from within. Paradoxically, little can be culled from the main alternative traditions—most relevantly socialism and its relative critical theory—without some reference back to liberalism. We are, for now, positioned on the edge of liberalism's lacuna with significant global threats at our backs. There are no ready-made instructions for cutting the captives loose and securing their freedom. Radical social movements, being both contestational *and* enmeshed, I will argue, are as close as we get. Their potential, while tentative, is the focus of this work.

This is also a book about the future of a modernity that having spread its wings is not particularly in focus—not to the intellectuals, not to the powerless, not even to the powerful—to the degree that they reflect upon the epochal at all. As an epoch, modernity heralded liberty, democracy, and scientific progress and is associated with industrialization and the free market. This work, however, is a studied reflection on the role of social movements in capitalist democracies during a period of intense academic debate as to whether we are witnessing a transition from

3

modernity to something else. It is this variously conceived yet widely shared sense that we are, in sociologist Alain Touraine's phrase, "leaving modernity,"[1] that gives the study of social movements new urgency. It is my argument that this perception of a shift is a recognition that certain elements of modernity are undermining the fundamentally political character of freedom that the new social movements (NSMs), however symbolically, have come to represent. Modernity, in this sense, is not a single integrated phenomenon but a complex and differentiated set of tendencies, some of which appear to be overwhelming others. The political modes of modernity—the rule of law, public accountability, and autonomy—are in retreat. The instrumental modes of modernity—concentrated capitalist accumulation, administrative rationality, natural resource exhaustion—are on the rise. Is this an inevitable loss? To slide over to such a view is to adopt, admittedly or not, a negative teleology. To suppose that democratic options remain, and to explore them in any empirical sense, is a tougher yet more urgent task.

My inquiry here is concerned with grasping the effects of the accumulation process and various institutional designs on our substantive rights as well as our reflexive capacities. In other words, it is, simultaneously, an inquiry into our contemporary experiences of freedom *and* into the question of whether markets and states today enlarge or threaten our ability to even contemplate those experiences in a coherent fashion. As such, it is also a testimony as to how very difficult it has become to think and talk about values, context, and practical possibilities in a logically related, accessible, and proactive fashion. This book is, no doubt, a salmon swimming upstream.

Ultimately, the project may be characterized as a political theoretical intervention from the position of practice. The subjects range from political and social theory to movement history; from institutional analysis to ideology, and from activism to the reflexive processes required to instigate change. Both the subject matter and my approach cross the often superficial boundaries of academic fields and even disciplines. As a result, my narrative sometimes struggles for consistency against the raging tides of terminological (and often, methodological) differences between (mostly) political science and sociology—both European and American. It is my hope, nonetheless, that I have made clear the political/theoretical tradition in which my thinking occurs and that I have defined my analytic categories and set out my conceptual priorities in a comprehensible manner.

THE ARGUMENT

In the post–1968 era, European and American observers of social movements began noting a shift in the forms, aims, and thinking of collective actors. Quick as academics are to discover something new, the term "new" social movement emerged as a reference to those social actors who, unlike their predecessors in the labor, socialist, and liberal rights-based movements of the nineteenth and twentieth centuries, were emphasizing new definitions of social relations in opposition to the market and the liberal state. The observance, of course, was just the beginning of a now 30-year debate over the verifiability, causes, meaning, and outcomes of the new forms.

My contribution here sides with the idea that the so-called new social movements are at least partially new. At the same time, I argue that while large-scale systemic developments are responsible for new patterns of collective engagement, the new forms depend to a significant degree on existing institutions and processes and, concomitantly, on ideological traditions, which vary considerably from nation to nation. In an effort to demonstrate that new patterns of collective engagement have indeed emerged in the post–World War II context *and* that those patterns are more or less constrained by national ideologies and institutional design, I have set out to investigate new social movement theory in the context of the United States. In this context I have discovered that the broader systemic imperatives—identified by many new social movement theorists as causal—combine with American ideological traditions and institutional constraints in such a way as to particularly handicap the new forms in the United States. Social movements have always had a hard time making headway in a nation where large-scale participatory democracy is disadvantaged. New macro developments in the economy and administration have only strengthened the force of these historical constraints; the primarily symbolic character of the new social movements under these circumstances is largely ephemeral. At the same time, I argue that whereas the conditioning force of systemic and national processes is intense, agency, or self-directed action, and the reflexive capacity of social movements are politically contingent and must be reasserted. Any such solution can greatly benefit from revisiting the basic categories of social and political theory in a sober effort to politically reconstruct an ideological orientation that is both radical and pragmatic, speculative and reflexive. Without such an undertaking, the new forms (especially in the United

States) will continue to move along the bifurcated trajectories of (1) deradicalization within the orbit of interest group liberalism, or (2) collapse along the periphery of power.

This book has essentially three parts: chapters 1 and 2 deal with social movement theory and political theory, while chapters 3, 4, and 5 examine the American context in light of claims identified in the first two chapters. In the conclusion I strive to construct a groundwork for a more reflexive movement ideology that might aid new social movements in dealing with the dilemmas highlighted throughout.

The first chapter of the book, "New Social Movements and Modernity: Continuity or Rupture?" is an overview of the definitions of a "new" social movement and seeks to identify the claim of newness in the context of social movement studies and contemporary social theory. Additionally, I conduct a more specific analysis of NSM theory. I frame my discussion by identifying two main trends in the literature, which I have divided simply as the "New Modernity theorists" and "Post Modernity theorists" of NSMs. The distinction is drawn in relation to the degree to which the theorists think that various Enlightenment notions associated with modernity continue to be both viable and valuable (i.e., universality, equality, rational modes of communication, and so on). While both groups of theorists argue that large-scale systemic and structural shifts are responsible for the emergence of NSMs (a rather modernist conception of history), the first group suggests that a potential for rational reflection persists among NSMs despite their noninstitutional character. The second group suggests that NSMs are fundamentally symbolic, cultural, and free from traditional modes of rationality.

Initially, I consider two New Modernity theorists: Claus Offe and Ulrich Beck (with reference also to Habermas). Their work, I contend, suggests that structural and systemic features have induced a new middle-class reflexivity, a new basis for politics, embodied in NSM. Second, I consider the work of Ernesto Laclau and Chantal Mouffe, Alberto Melucci, and Alain Touraine as suggestive of a shift away from or break with modernity in which NSMs are offered as evidence of an integrated symbolic system of social meaning in which definitional struggles occur in symbolic terms.

I consider Offe and Beck's contentions that NSMs emerge in the context of the Keynesian welfare state and "technoeconomic progress" respectively. I also consider their common claim that NSMs are composed largely of people from the margins of the middle class. I then evaluate the

Post Modernity theorists' claim that the core social movement conflicts are located in the cultural or symbolic sphere. I investigate how both these approaches thematize the gulf between the radical promises of NSMs and the actual outcomes. Finally I suggest that the New Modernity theorists, while insufficiently thematizing the relationship between actual movement outcomes in the context of the modernizing forces they suggest underpin them, offer greater potential than the Post Modernity theories.

In chapter 2, "Reason, Politics, and Social Movements," I seek to make clear the normative and theoretical concerns that frame my entire discussion of NSMs in the United States. While the title of my book suggests that these NSMs are caught in a bind, it is my most basic assumption that while this indeed may be descriptively true, it need not remain so. In response to the gap between descriptions and outcomes evident in the New Modernity theories of social movements, I investigate the role of politics traditionally conceived in gauging the self-understandings and effectiveness of social movements.

While my critique of actual NSM practices and ideology in America takes place later, in chapter 4 on the U.S. student movement (1985–1992), in this second chapter I am ultimately making the claim that for democratic social movements in our era, there are certain indispensable and normatively inspired practices, which both originate in and are simultaneously threatened by forces unleashed with the Enlightenment. Sorting out these contrary forces based on an interest in the recovery and expansion of democratic practice is in many respects the most difficult yet necessary task for any critical social theory with a positive intent. I begin this discussion with an emphasis on the contingent aspects of social movements. I stress the practical necessity of distinguishing between social movements on the right and left. The contemporary situation of capitalist democracies suggests that new movements, while sharing a distance from traditional politics and an emphasis on identity, present vastly different ideological and normative interests. As such, the self-directed action of social movements relies on interpretation and emphasizes the role of ideology. At the same time, systemic conditions underpin a more generalized dissatisfaction with and alienation from traditional politics. I suggest that systemic shifts go a long way in accounting for the emergence of new kinds of conflict, but they do not (and could not) exhaustively account for the self-understanding and normative goals of participants.

The irony for NSM theory may be that movements like the grass roots of the Christian Right appear more pronounced than their more egalitarian counterparts. This observation, coupled with the demands of globalization (i.e., more centralized, less accountable economic and political decision making), suggests that the loss of meaning that traditional politics presents for ordinary people hardly signals a more emancipatory age. Indeed, conditions like these threaten the institutional preconditions for the expression of progressive social movements in the first place. As such, I argue that progressive social movements have an inherent interest in the pragmatic recovery, reform, and transformation of liberalism's most expansive elements.

The need for democratic social movements to recover elements from the liberal tradition assumes that this is possible from a position of practice, and not simply a matter of theory. In this sense, sociology has helped to emphasize the functional role of social structures and to elucidate the ways that certain liberal norms and practices are disappearing from civil society. But political theory can help us understand the responsibility that emerges from nonfunctionalist world views. A sociological argument may enlighten us as to the ways that structural developments become socialized through institutions, but political theory reminds us that it works in reverse as well. And when we view political theory as both a reflexive and speculative enterprise, the importance of establishing binding political criteria emerges. In this sense, an historical look at the way liberal political theory has justified binding norms can help clarify two things for social movements today: (1) despite the falsity of grounding schemes, identifiable norms and procedures were considered fundamental to democratic governance by those aiming for political transformation, and (2) accountability and public control in our era cannot be conceived of without appropriating and reconstructing the political (but not metaphysical) elements of these democratic norms and procedures.

Reason, I will argue, has served as an ideological anchor for liberal norms over the last three centuries. By way of a discussion of Hobbes, Kant, and Dewey, I sketch three distinct conceptualizations of reason as a foundation for liberal and democratic practice. Regardless of the imaginary grounding schemes offered, I suggest that modern political theory's near obsession with reason ultimately reveals a contingent yet fundamental relationship between egalitarian norms, a notion of shared, intersubjective capacities, and universal democratic procedures for debate. This is not to suggest that theory dictates practice, but that ideas do indeed become institutionalized and socialized through the efforts of political movements. My aim is to point out that the eventual institutionalization of liberal democratic norms, *however inconsistently and hypocritically,* has conditioned the pragmatic understandings of ordinary citizens and has historically given way to demands for greater freedom and justice. What appears as reason in the canons of political theory can most fruitfully be exposed as normative and procedural demands aiming for political institutionalization. While capitalist industrialization and the rise of the administrative state have, to a significant degree, undermined the substantive realization of the egalitarian promise of liberalism's reason, its political character requires reasserting. The potential for recovering and transforming liberalism's democratic promise must begin with efforts to bring the undermining forces under democratic control. That possibility rests on operationalizing on a mass public scale, something akin to what Jurgen Habermas has so insightfully and keenly thematized as "communicative action." Our only vehicles for such a reassertion are radical social movements.

The rest of chapter 2 focuses on Habermas's contribution to understanding NSMs by way of a discussion of reason as communicative action, and his notion of the public sphere. Ultimately, while embracing the theoretical and normative direction of his work, I suggest that its usefulness lies in connecting it to empirical movements and their potential for developing communicative action within a given context. Whereas Habermas's theory of differentiated rationalities resulting from systemic processes allows us to focus on social movements as a potential site for halting the further encroachment of democratic practice, the generality of his account requires that variations in "welfare mass democracies" (at the level of both the state and national ideology) must first be thematized before the practical potential of communicative action can be gauged. I will later suggest that in order for communicative action to gain credible ideological weight in relation to countering the effects of the accumulation process, the adoption by social movements of what Stephen Bronner has called a "class ethic" is indispensable.[2]

On the general observation that NSMs are both systemic in character and yet significantly shaped by variations in national contexts, I begin part two by focusing on the historical resistance to progressive social movements in the American context. Chapter 3 ("Locke, Stock, and Barricades") begins a discussion of the particular constraints presented to NSM formations in the United States by way of a historical discussion of the American ideological and institutional context. Here I evaluate Louis Hartz's thesis regarding the impact of Lockian liberalism as well as the legacy of Hamilton and Madison on institutional designs. The institutional concerns of both Madison and Hamilton of limiting popular control and the impact of "factions" has significantly contributed to the historical development of social movement postures and positions. In addition, I consider the impact of the lack of socialist success in the United States and review various theories of American exceptionalism. The original institutional and ideological constraints on social movement challenges from below, I claim, negatively affected the modes of challenge that were to emerge over the next 150 years.

Institutional adaptations, such as the emergence of the two-party system and attendant electoral restraints, contributed to a set of social movement patterns that reinscribed the old limits on popular movements seeking to affect centers of power. In particular, I highlight the interplay between three historic social movements (socialism, populism, and the progressive movement) and the American state in light of the limits of both institutional arrangements and liberal ideology. By focusing on the interplay, I seek to demonstrate the legacies (both institutional and ideological) for subsequent social movements. Later I will argue that the further development of constraints after the Great Depression were in no small measure foreshadowed in the electoral arrangements and attendant justification that developed in response to these three historic movements.

Chapter 4 begins by relating the rise of interest-group liberalism in the post–New Deal era, with the rise of symbolic and cultural politics among social movements. Whereas important social welfare guarantees are secured while pursuing Keynesian economic policy, institutional (administrative) developments in the United States occurred in the context of a constrained electoral system that ultimately heightened the symbolic radicalism of social movements. Systemic developments take on a particular form in the United States, which paradoxically both underpin *and* further marginalize radical social movement efforts. The development of what Theodore Lowi has called "interest-group liberalism" ultimately produces a context in which administration overwhelms representation and accountability. The particular character of the administrative state in the United States can also be read as a double-edged sword; ultimately it is a strategic response to the popular challenges that agitated for and won limited welfare guarantees in a context of decreased mechanisms of public control. As such, it is a response that continues in the spirit of Hamilton, Madison, and Lockian liberalism. In turn, these responses have contributed to the conditioning of social movement repertoires in a way that works against a critical understanding of the institutional and ideological context in which movements become enmeshed. For example, necessary welfare guarantees themselves become associated with the intrusive administrative rationality against which NSMs rail.

The effects condition movements to see themselves in relation to one of two ideological orientations: strategic action (interest groups) or symbolic radicalism (identity politics). It is in this context that the discussion of social movement repertoires continues. The emergence of NSM practice in the United States is related to choices made by 1960s movements in a context that was uniquely constrained by continued ideological traditions and new institutional developments. The combined effects have tended to bifurcate the path open to social movements, sending movements down one of two roads—interest group politics or symbolic action. Here I focus on three defining moments in 1960s social movement history. The moments selected illustrate the bifurcated pattern. Here three groups unwilling to be drawn into the orbit of interest group politics define themselves against the integrating processes by emphasizing a radical, symbolic posture. The move is illustrated by (1) the rise of black power in the Student Nonviolent Coordinating Committee, (2) the cultural turn associated with the Yippies, and (3) the identity-based concerns of the radical women's liberation movement. I argue that the degree to which movements rely merely on symbolic politics and identity-based ideologies is the degree to which movements are denied access to formal institutions. In weighing available choices, I suggest that a shift to the cultural ground represented an attempt to maintain a radical politics in a context of institutional exclusion. At the same time, I caution that while such a turn may indeed be pragmatic from time to time, it is a costly one, especially when turned into a reified ideological code. Such a choice must be reflexively adopted not as an end in itself, but as a means of gaining critical momentum for institutional reform. Such reflexivity presupposes an ideological orientation that can navigate both strategic and symbolic modes based on identifiable and shared interests. In this regard, I discuss a theme here and again in the next chapter—namely that the economic agenda and ideological features evident in Martin Luther King's later work offer a tradition that NSMs would indeed do well to revisit. To the degree that the Rainbow Coalition picked up on this tradition in the context of 1980s social movements was a promising—albeit ultimately disappointing—reminder of the necessity of democratic structures and procedures and the power of a class ethic for social movements today.

The three movement moments selected reflect the roots of NSM ideology in the United States and are historical references for current dilemma. Unfortunately, much of NSM theory itself does not contribute to a reflexive basis for activists to sort through such moments and ends up glossing over significant defeats.

Chapter 5 initiates a closer look at a more current new social movement example—the 1980s student movement. I frame the discussion in the context of the weakness of NSM theory as developed to this point and attempt to illustrate the limits and failures of the kind of practice NSM theory often enshrines. By selecting two critical junctures in the 1980s student movement in which students were presented with the possibility of asserting themselves as a more organized force, I demonstrate how the diffuse movement was unable to navigate the challenge. As a result, the movement fell into a general state of disarray and virtual collapse. I then evaluate my claim regarding outcomes (collapse v. integration). In this chapter, I establish the complexities facing actual movements and emphasize the need for NSMs themselves to theorize about their context. Picking up on the theme introduced above regarding the radical Civil Rights tradition, I suggest that within the 1980s student movement, the degree to which those steeped in this tradition were in leadership positions was the degree of promise. Where these students and their organizations were ignored or overwhelmed by other ideological orientations and individuals is where the bifurcated pattern reemerges—identity politics v. interest-group behavior. As such, I emphasize the need to adopt processes and norms that avoid adopting either strategic or symbolic modes exclusively. In the American context, an orientation of this kind, in broad ideological terms, will be associated with the universalism, accountability, and class ethic of the radical Civil Rights tradition. Also identified in this section are the types of ideological and political challenges that an adequate theory needs to take into consideration to help NSMs in America thematize not only the American context but also the large-scale forces they seek to contest.

Finally, in chapter 6, I conclude by suggesting an alternative framework for social movement analysis that builds on the systemic and structural concerns of NSM theory, while simultaneously valuing the role of political institutions and ideology in mediating social movement formations and outcomes. Here the contributions of Habermas are recalled.

I agree here with Habermas that two main differentiated but overlapping forces of modernization are evident in the accumulation process and in the administrative state. While taking up Habermas's view of social movements as anchored in but uncoupled from these processes, I suggest that for communicative action to be real, social movements must not only adopt normative procedures that are universal, rational, and democratic, they must also gauge concerns reflexively in relation to undermining forces. This, I suggest, is particularly difficult in the American context, where pragmatic understandings are influenced by the "stubborn constraints" thematized in chapter 2.

Nonetheless, it is exactly these stubborn constraints that require attention. Both the accumulation process and the modern state require critical evaluation by NSMs so that demands and actions not be subject to the same bifurcating pattern I described earlier. With respect to the accumulation process, I draw on Stephen Bronner's "class ethic" as a way that otherwise disparate NSMs might ideologically orient strategic demands to expand besieged welfare state functions—functions that can potentially generate greater publicness among the poor and lessen obstacles to a more genuine public sphere. While calling free-market principles into question, welfare demands support silenced people. At the same time, the adoption of a class ethic might prove to be a basis for generating alliances between social movements and challenge the fragmentation associated with identity politics.

With respect to the state, I draw on the political and institutional concerns of Piven and Cloward and suggest that the electoral-representative system is crucial to social movement outcomes. By maintaining an orientation to the state that emphasizes how the electoral-representative system constrains NSMs, participants may simultaneously advocate reforms of the system that will lessen the de-radicalizing impact of strategic action. Challenging the electoral laws around campaign finance as well as the two-party system itself will help. But such an eye on the political process is limited without the broader ideological perspective provided by NSMs that have reflexively adopted the politics of a class ideal. In conjunction, these elements may give meaning to the deeply felt but politically inchoate sentiments evident in contemporary U.S. social movements and provide for increased impact.

NSMs have a unique role to play in the democratic reform of increasingly undemocratic institutions, but only if they adopt a more reflexive movement ideology and strategies, tactics, and organizational forms that aim for increasing the mechanisms of control against the undermining forces of modernization. While exceedingly difficult to do in practice, it is nonetheless practically imperative.

NOTES

1. See Alain Touraine's *Critique of Modernity* (Cambridge, Mass.: Blackwell, 1995).
2. See Stephen Bronner's *Socialism Unbound* (New York: Routledge, 1989).

Chapter One

New Social Movements and Modernity: Continuity or Rupture?

WHAT IS A NEW SOCIAL MOVEMENT ANYWAY?

In the summer of 1993, as I was just beginning my research on this project, I came across an article in a popular New York weekly that captured the promise and problems of a "typical" new social movement (NSM). There, the widely hailed NSM group, Women's Action Coalition, was practically elegized. The headline read "WAC Attacks Itself: Will the Direct Action Group Self Destruct?"[1] The Women's Action Coalition, based in New York City, initially made headlines because of its creative use of symbolic tactics in raising women's issues in response to Supreme Court abortion rights restrictions in 1991. But WAC's agenda, like most NSMs, cannot be captured in the traditional political language of rights. The project can be more accurately captured in its emphasis on autonomy, substantive equality, and a new communalism constructed through collective action aiming for, in this case, the transformation of gender relations. Unlike the nineteenth-century suffrage movement, and perhaps even more unlike their contemporary liberal counterparts, such as the feminist interest group National Abortion Rights Action League (NARAL), WAC stood for radical transformation and not inclusion or integration. Indeed, what makes a new social movement new, according to most observers, is the refusal to be satisfied with a justice defined by the limits, protections, or formal procedures associated with the liberal state. Grasping at a not-yet-realized freedom, NSMs are engaged in what Herbert Marcuse called the "great refusal."

With respect to vision, tactics, and organizational structures, NSMs seek to contest authoritarianism in its many and varied social, cultural, and political guises. In this regard, WAC was typical: Not only did the group's vision emphasize autonomy, so too did their action styles and group procedures. WAC was self-identified as a decentralized "zap" action group, whose meetings were open and where decision making was decidedly antihierarchical. It is a picture that mostly fits the descriptions offered by various social theorists beginning in the mid-1970s. At about this time, groups of social movement observers, primarily European, began generalizing about what were perceived as new trends in protest since the 1960s. Most of the new academic explanations seemed to converge on at least one point: Contemporary social protest demonstrated a move away from the liberal state as an arena of bargaining. Soon the term new social movement caught on despite significantly different accounts of the origins and meanings of the new trends.

As the literature grew, additional postures and attitudes became associated with the new waves of protest. To offer one theorist's characterizations, in NSMs, "multitudes of individuals become collective actors [in] highly informal, ad hoc, discontinuous, context-sensitive, and egalitarian modes."[2] Varieties of NSM theories seemed to be converging on some similar observations, which emphasized three elements: a primary emphasis on noneconomic forms of injustice; a rejection of traditional political modes of protest associated with the labor movement, parties, or interest groups; and a concern with the "symbolic" content of demands and actions. Certainly, groups like WAC fit such specifications.

Whereas the descriptions seemed, to a large degree, to be broadly demonstrable, the causes and the outcomes of such a phenomena remained variously conceived, hotly contested, or simply unclear in the literature. While NSM theorists seemed to be connecting the new forms to progressive social change, actual social transformation proved difficult to validate. In the case of WAC, the increasing resonance of its message, and the growth that ensued, actually proved debilitating. That popular growth is a traditional measure of social movement success did not square with the experience of WAC or many other American NSMs. Growth, at least in the American context, frequently seemed to invite sudden death.

By 1992, local WAC meetings in New York City drew anywhere from 150 to 300 participants. Yet by 1993, WAC had plummeted in membership, focus, and confidence. Given my own background in U.S. social movements from 1984 to 1992, the cycle of success, growth, and implosion was disappointingly familiar. The not-yet-two-year-old shooting star of direct action politics seemed to embody many of the fundamental dilemmas facing NSM formations in the United States today. Likewise, WAC experienced crises in leadership, organizational continuity, and agenda setting. While WAC demonstrated many of the features NSM theorists attribute to the new forms of social challenge, their ability to sustain action was limited.

WAC's nonhierarchical structure, open membership, encouragement of split-off actions, and preference for media-oriented and symbolic politics are typical of many NSMs. But the free-floating leadership and decision-making processes made organizational continuity difficult. When success visits such a group by way of increased numbers of participants (as it did in the case of WAC) the meanings, strategies, and aims can become blurry. The vision, loosely premised on the not yet realized, makes the projection of a unified agenda or identity difficult. Under such circumstances, it is understandable that ideological coherence becomes more difficult to project, especially when, as a matter of principle, internal decisions are neither formal nor binding. The internal dynamics of mobilization and self-understanding in groups like WAC implies an ideology and practice that seem to present obstacles to accountability, stability, and impact.

For those who theorize about social movements, the new forms also presented a variety of challenges. NSM theorists, it appears, have correctly detected a new sensibility among social movements. At the same time, varieties of NSM theorists impute a counter-hegemonic effect to the new forms, which the WAC example would seem to contradict. In more traditional social movement studies, the explanation for such lack of impact can usually be teased out of an analysis that emphasizes the availability and strategic uses of resources in relation to centers of power—or in Mancur Olson's phrase, "the logic of collective action." For example, in considering the case of WAC, it might be suggested that organizational confusion led to the inefficient use of resources, or perhaps that WAC had failed to take advantage of strategic opportunities presented by electoral arrangements, lobbying, or other power alliances. Despite the degree of explanatory power such movement analysis offers, NSMs by definition resist the implications of these calculations. What NSMs and their observers have done is to call the old categories into question. If NSMs are indeed engaging in the "great refusal," and forming themselves in opposition to the status quo, then explanations that attribute their failures to not playing the game well enough beg that question. At the same time, theorists who celebrate those aspects of NSM that break with the logic of the system seem oblivious to the limited potential implied by actual out-comes—outcomes that demonstrate marginal and highly tentative effects on the everyday lives of ordinary people.

Because much of the NSM literature was both European-based and largely optimistic about outcomes, in the course of my research I began to suspect that perhaps the new trend was mediated by other factors that might be national or regional in character. Does European NSM theory assume a national context that is less constrained, both ideologically and institutionally, than the United States? Are the political implications of NSMs related to differences in, for example, the electoral system as well as welfare–state functions? Is the characteristic of fluidity more pronounced among U.S. movements or just more vulnerable here given the institutional and ideological restraints of the American system? These questions led me to ask whether the NSM cycle with which I was familiar (symbolic action, growth, collapse), was in some way "exceptional" in the American sense. Furthermore, what might be the implications of such a claim for social movement theory generally? To even pose these questions, however, I found myself taking a critical and more empirical step back from some of the abstractions that operate in much of NSM theory. My central question became, what, in theoretical terms, was responsible for NSM theory's seemingly accurate descriptions of broad trends, but its failure to account for actual outcomes?

By posing these questions, I have undertaken a project that is both theoretical and practical: concerned with squaring, so to speak, the abstract and the real while holding to the normative interests that have informed the inquiry from the outset—political, social, and economic justice and accountability. Considering my interests this project is, at heart, a theoretical intervention from the position of practice. It is an intervention that, from an intellectual point of view, must begin by exploring the categories embedded in not simply new social movement theory, but contemporary social theory generally.

CONTEMPORARY SOCIAL MOVEMENT THEORY

In the winter of 1985, the journal *Social Research* published a watershed issue on social movements under the interpretive eye of guest editor Jean Cohen. In that one issue, the central ideas of four of the most influential social movement thinkers—Tilly, Touraine, Melucci, and Offe—were captured in some signature articles. The journal inspired renewed academic inquiry into social movements at a time when significant progressive resistance in an otherwise conservative climate was being noted globally.

In the lead article, Cohen carved her theoretical task by comparing the two main competing paradigms in the field of social movement studies: resource mobilization theory (RMT)—largely American on the one hand—and NSM theory—largely European on the other. From that comparison, Cohen suggested that despite their differences, the two paradigms could inform each other. She also noted that "each involves a theoretical framework that excludes the main focus of the other."[3] While the debate between RMT and NSM theories arose out of the attempt to explain new forms of collective action since the mid-seventies, the debate refers the reader back to contemporary social theory's most basic categories. In so doing, this debate has raised important questions regarding the coherence of theoretical, methodological, and normative assumptions and how they square with empirical cases. It is little wonder that this debate continues to inspire researchers, theorists, and activists alike.

As both a participant in the movements characterized in that literature and as an intellectual interested in social theories that seemed to be moving social movements to the center of an analysis aiming for the political and social transformation of capitalist democracies, I have quite naturally been drawn to the debate. Cohen's observation, some fifteen years ago, that these two paradigms each had something to offer that the other was missing is a problematic not easily traversed. The debates suggested that RMT provided a realistic and necessary understanding of the strategic dimensions of social movements; NSM theory, on the other hand, emphasized the normative or ideological value (or nonstrategic elements) embedded in the new forms. Like Cohen, I believe that these divergent approaches cannot be satisfactorily squared through synthesis or by an ad hoc accounting of the respective missing elements. Instead, in order to consider the competing claims that social movements might be both new in a contestational, prefigurative sense, and yet also be tied to strategic rationality, requires a critical theoretical position that simply breaks the boundaries of RMT.

RMT can be broadly identified as an approach that, in contrast to its "parent" collective behavior approach, emphasizes the institutional logic of social conflict.[4] Employing what can generally be termed as a conflict model of collective action, RMT emphasizes the costs and benefits of—and the opportunities for—action. As a second wave of RM theorists have put it, "By treating the activities of collective actors as tactics and strategy, the analyst could examine movements and counter-movements as engaged in a rational game to achieve specific interests, much like the pluralist competition among interest groups in political analysis."[5] The emphasis is placed on deciding between options for the maximization of calculated interests.

NSM theory, a more difficult approach to characterize generally, can be painted as a post–sixties theoretical response to what appeared to be new forms of collective action that frustrated the assumptions of RMT. Taking its cue from the emergence of movements that emphasized a concern with identity, ecology, autonomy, and culture, NSM theories are most frequently premised on systemic accounts of modernization, which posit that the perceived fluid, symbolic, and nonstrategic character of the NSMs signals an emancipatory shift away from dominant institutions and integrating rationalities. This observation is conceived in significantly different ways by authors as diverse as Jurgen Habermas and Alberto Melucci. But, broadly speaking, NSM theory places value on movements retaining a normative and ideological distance from the center.

In the past fifteen years there has been a type of dialogue between proponents of RMT and NSM theory. As a result of the issues raised by NSM theory, representatives in each approach have tried to account for their respective weaknesses without abandoning their basic frameworks. These two approaches, as Cohen warned, suffer from opposite problems: On the one hand, RMT as a theory of organizational strategy and tactics methodologically enshrines a kind of strategic rationality thought to be eschewed by NSMs. NSM theories, on the other hand, usually provide metatheoretical accounts that impute to new forms a systemic–counter-systemic character that is broadly descriptive but, empirically speaking, questionable. In this sense, RM theorists have had to account for the counter-logic of "new" social movement norms, ideologies, and procedures. NSM theorists have had to contend with an opposite problem: The empirical verification of the claim that nonstrategic movements are both prolific and contestational has proved elusive. Indeed, the central claim of some NSM theorists that collective conflict has shifted from political arenas to the more elusive cultural and symbolic arena exacerbates the problem of validation.

Earlier I suggested that in trying to understand the prefigurative as well as strategic dimensions of NSM, it is imperative to step back from RMT. By taking this position, I am arguing that an adequate social movement theory must first be willing and able to distinguish between the normative, systemic (structural), and contingent aspects of social life in contemporary capitalist democracies.[6] By this I mean that it is crucial that social theory retain separate but coherently related moments of analysis for the distinct logics of ideology (both within movements themselves and the broader society), structural constraints, and political arrangements. In this respect, NSM theory, while frequently overly general and rashly optimistic, provides a better starting point than RMT. Whereas RMT ultimately ties social movements to the logic of structural and state administrative demands, some of what NSM theory has to offer provides an opportunity for a significant reworking based on its shortcomings.

Despite more recent attention paid to the role of ideology and norms on the part of many innovative RM theorists,[7] the various efforts to graft accounts of the nonstrategic elements of NSMs onto a theory of strategic action fail to account for the privileged role of strategic action in the first place. Moreover, from this perspective the normative and ideological orientation of progressive movements are reduced to "resources"; the relationship between norms and the systemic field, be it mimetic, reflexive, or reactionary, eludes the framework.

Among the most sophisticated analyses to be lumped in with the RMT approach is the work of Charles Tilly.[8] Tilly argues for the historical emergence of strategic action repertoires on the part of social movements as a response to the rise of the capitalist market economy and the nation–state. In so doing, Tilly provides a partial account of why strategic action becomes analytically privileged in movement studies. But, as I argue in subsequent chapters, successful U.S. movements along this model usually suffer the deradicalization of nonstrategic demands—especially those demands tied to economic transformation. The price of success is a neutralized vision: movements unwilling to surrender their radical vision simply fade away.

Like Tilly's, the work of Frances Fox Piven and Richard Cloward on poor movements by the people in the United States provides a critical account of how capitalist imperatives structure political institutions and social movement developments. Piven and Cloward, no doubt, are unparalleled in their thematization of movements and the American political process. It is their work on both movements by the poor as well as electoral politics that persuasively identifies the electoral and socioeconomic conditions under which social movements are more likely to have an impact. At the same time, their argument suggests that radical social movements are inevitably trumped by state and economic demands. Progress is intermittent at best, limited, and always tentative because movements must remain nonparliamentary actors to retain their influence. Social movements in the work of Piven and Cloward are ultimately consigned to the margins where they serve as important but ultimately weak correctives to system functions. In the works of Tilly and Piven and Cloward, the integrating logic of the political process leave the critical potential of NSMs out in the cold. Ultimately, disruption substitutes for transformation.

Nonetheless, many scholars coming out of this tradition have provided enormously rich empirical accounts of social movements and their interaction with the state—accounts that are few and far between in NSM literature. For my purposes here, and to the degree that I retain an interest in thematizing the impact of the political process on movement formation and outcomes, I frequently rely on the accounts of these scholars. At the same time, I suggest that the logic of the system can be resisted and transformed by NSMs in ways unexplored in that literature. This claim follows from a reworking of the observation by some NSM theorists that new social movements are not simply a petulant or hopelessly utopian rejection of "rationality" but represent a potential for recovery of a repressed use of critical public reason once associated with, but no longer evident in, democratic institutions and parliamentary procedures. With this criteria in mind, it may be more obvious why I'm arguing that RMT will simply not provide an adequate basis for analysis. Instead, from the perspective of movements' potential for a recovery or expansion of democratic practice—as opposed to bargaining successfully or maximizing pressure on the system—my general tack has been to investigate the shortcomings of NSM theory in the context of American institutions and ideologies.

My efforts here begin by sharing with NSM theorists a general concern with thematizing the systemic dimensions of modernization, specifically resulting from the accumulation process and administrative state functions. Like many NSM theorists, I argue that modernization processes have substantially severed the public from critical access to the institutions and processes that administer their lives. But in my view, NSM theory has two distinct approaches. One posits that NSMs evidence a fundamental break with modernity and key features associated with politics traditionally conceived. The other argues that differentiated notions of rationality are present under modernization, suggesting that NSMs are capable of being both contestational and simultaneously continuous with modernity. I refer to these approaches below as Post Modernity and New Modernity theories of social movements, respectively.

Because I also bring to my analysis a normative interest in recovering and expanding those besieged elements of modernity embedded in the promise of representative democracy, my inquiry and argument throughout is concerned with the potential of the New Modernity theories of social movements. Beginning with the contributions of Jurgen Habermas, I suggest that such a recovery proceeds from the pragmatic and simultaneously normative identification of a repressed use of critical reason that is potentially evident in NSMs. As such, I also assume that the viability of the contemporary liberal–welfare state as an arena for significant reform has not been exhausted to the point of irrelevance for progressive social movements.

The criteria of recovering democratic practice necessarily refers social movements, however critically, back to the state.[9] My assertion contradicts some of the central claims of NSM theory, which purport the waning significance of the state to social movement outcomes. NSM theories, to the degree that they celebrate the new forms as anti-statist, fail to admit the vulnerability of new forms. This is particularly evident in the American context.

While my rejection of RMT as a useful paradigm is premised on my observation that its assumptions shut out the reflexive potential of NSMs, I am also critical of NSM theory but in less fundamental ways. Whereas much of NSM theory suggests that social transformation (and, for that matter, prior reflexive awareness) is endemic to the NSM form itself, the character and outcome of NSMs are largely variable, and, as such, open to question. In addition, NSMs must pay attention to the institutional preconditions for their own expression and expansion; this understanding should direct NSMs toward the political reassertion and expansion of besieged electoral and welfare guarantees. These threatened elements of the modern liberal state offer the needed basis for future contributions of progressive social movements. As such, NSMs need to reflexively thematize their *strategic* relationship to the state and dominant ideology while retaining their radical vision. NSMs require a reflexive awareness of the political process (in a context of systemic tendencies), with the hope that they can develop practical responses to the conditioning effects of institutional and ideological constraints. This cannot be accomplished without the self-created understandings and practices of NSMs themselves.

While much of my argument stems from the contributions made by Jurgen Habermas regarding the potential for communicative action that NSMs represent, I bring to those insights the desire to enliven and contextualize what is a fundamentally abstract and largely procedural accounting of NSM potential. Toward that end, I am interested in establishing the significance of variations in institutional and ideological contexts among welfare mass democracies in deciphering NSM outcomes. My approach emphasizes that within a systemic context the possibilities for action frames vary considerably. By emphasizing movements' self-understandings in a mixed context of systemic, institutional, and ideological constraints, a more empirical, more practical groundwork for communicative action usefulness might be distinguished.

WHITHER THE STATE? WHITHER CLASS? THE RASH PREDICTIONS OF NSM THEORY

NSM theory has emerged in response to the proliferation of new trends in Europe and North America among social movement formations in the post–1968 era. One of the tenets of NSM theory is that these trends are in fact new. What appears to be new in NSM is that new conflicts, on the Left or the Right, position themselves against both traditional politics and the influence of economic elites. While Habermas has suggested that new conflicts are emerging around "quality of life, equality, individual self-realization, participation, and human rights"[10] issues, he also suggests that the ideological and normative orientation of these movements is not pre-ordained by systemic processes. There is, so to speak, nothing automatic about the normative dimensions of NSMs.

Much of the literature assumes that new conflicts evidence a progressive egalitarian orientation. Indeed, definitionally, NSM as a term has come to refer exclusively to progressive, radical efforts. In addition, much of the literature confers upon these progressive ascriptions a contestational quality. Yet the very characteristics heralded by NSM theorists as contestational ultimately prove to be problematic for NSMs in the American context. Furthermore, certain ascribed characteristics have the effect of severely limiting NSM outcomes in the American context, including (1) a contradictory stance toward the state—demonstrated by seeking resources and redress from the state while promulgating an anti-statist, anti-bureaucratic politic; (2) an emphasis on the prefigurative, which manifests itself as the demand for adherence to highly egalitarian social norms and organizational structures that prove to be shifting, indeterminate, and nonaccountable; and (3) the replacement of a failed Marxist teleology with identity politics, which ultimately reduces questions of economics, politics, and ideology to cultural struggles based on experience and location, thus undermining potential bases for solidarity. While among the New Modernity theorists there are concerns about unity and the relationship of NSMs to state power,[11] overdrawn systemic assumptions eclipse the degree to which NSMs' impact is related to certain institutional and ideological traditions.

While each of the three characteristics stipulated above challenges the old paradigm associated with the working-class and anti-imperialist struggles of the late nineteenth and early- to mid-twentieth centuries, they prove ineffective, particularly when considered in the American institutional context. Ultimately, while the challenge of NSMs justifiably reflect the inadequacy of the old paradigm as well as changing historical conditions, their practices present profound political problems, particularly in the American context. There, NSMs either adopt excessively symbolic postures or are absorbed into the complex of interest-group behavior, thus truncating their radical impulses. For those social movements thwarted by systemic and institutional constraints, the turn inward, with the accompanying emphasis on the prefigurative, often produces antidemocratic, unaccountable, and nonegalitarian practices, which offer no viable counter to the dominant arrangements. On the other hand, those social movements that adopt strategic (as opposed to symbolic) politics illustrate the powerful lure of interest-group liberalism. In this case the critical, radical quality of NSMs is overwhelmed.

NSM rhetoric and intraorganizational practice evidence a rejection of the idea of the expanded modern state on the grounds that it is inherently oppressive. Yet reliance by NSMs on the state for resources, concessions, and, perhaps most importantly, for the protection of expression, reveals an inadequate and contradictory conception of power and politics. The popular NSM paradigm—known as identity politics or the politics of dominance—fails to distinguish between different types of hierarchies (e.g., social movement v. corporate hierarchy; accountable v. authoritarian hierarchies) and, as a result, many NSMs operate, both in practice and rhetorically, as if the economy, the state, and social relations are equivalent forms of dominance. Popular wisdom among NSM adherents today reflects the idea that, for example, the welfare state, class analysis, and the call for a national confederation of single-issue organizations are all expressions of dominance. The attachment to localized, single-issue formations, to the exclusion of national multi-issue organizing, does not herald a new era of counter-hegemonic formations—rather it indicates a need for reconceptualizing transformation. NSM theory, therefore, should also benefit from a reformulation which, in response to actual NSM outcomes, I believe begins by thematizing the systemic dimensions of social life (i.e., the accumulation process and administrative state functions), while providing for the reflexive distance of subjects able to reach a collective understanding of their context. More than that, interests, constraints, and ideological or normative dimensions of social movements must be formulated by participants in such a frame.

While much of what has been referred to here under the title NSM theory shares in a general effort to value the new modes of collective action, enormous differences are simultaneously glossed over by such a categorization. These differences are not just a matter of intellectual interest, but to the degree that social theory has anything to contribute to an actual movement's ability to reconstruct democratic practice, these differences are significant.

Below I divide NSM theory into two general camps: New Modernity and Post Modernity theories. Of course, there are many other ways to compare and contrast the authors represented. But my distinction is based on the degree to which the theorists assume that an actual break with modernity as well as its political ideals, institutions, and ways of knowing (i.e., equality, representative democracy, reason) is evident and welcomed in the new forms. Because much of NSM theory suggests that the new forms stand in contrast to the negative aspects of modernization, the question remains whether elements of modernity are retained in the new forms, or whether something wholly new has emerged. Whether new forms are partially new (as I believe) or wholly new, it remains essential to identify how movements might establish binding norms and institutional accountability.

It is my argument below that the degree to which social movement theorists assume that modernization processes present one homogenizing, debilitating logic is also the degree to which NSMs come to symbolize a break with the old. Whether it is as rupture (as in Laclau and Mouffe) or as contestants in the central epochal struggle (i.e., Reason v. Subjectivation in Touraine), Post Modernity theories are, I believe, those positions that concede democratically relevant features of modernity (reason, the modern state, universalism) to the negative forces of modernization. I suggest that by fudging a systemic or counter-systemic relationship between the old and the new, the normative and ideological dimensions of NSM are reduced, by way of an overwrought and disguised form of functionalism, to an ambiguous symbolic radicalism that is doomed to fail. The New Modernity theories are those which describe a differentiated logic of modernization that opens up the possibility not only for continuity with democratically valuable aspects of modernity, but suggest that NSMs' self-understandings are a source of critical reflection and agency. While ultimately I suggest that New Modernity theorists are weak in understanding the relationship between critical agency and the political context, their insights into systemic constraints and the relevance of modernity's democratic controls make them a more useful starting point for social movements today.

THE NEW MODERNITY
THEORISTS OF NEW SOCIAL MOVEMENTS

We are witnessing not the end but the beginning of modernity—that is, of a modernity beyond its classical industrial design.

Ulrich Beck, *Risk Society*

Ulrich Beck and Claus Offe, two representatives of New Modernity theories of social movements, have made significant contributions to the study of social movements. Beck and Offe, using different strategies, attempt to reformulate critical social theory in an effort to link emancipatory politics to economic, political, and ideological shifts. Not unlike the work of Jurgen Habermas, Beck and Offe are concerned with overcoming the negative consequences of instrumental rationality as formulated by the Frankfurt School figures. Habermas's body of work is dedicated to recapturing democratic practice for an increasingly eclipsed public. Discontent with the "negative dialectic" of his teachers (Adorno and Horkheimer), Habermas forwards a theoretical construction of a universalist and normative basis for political action. His notion of universalism rests on a concept of reflexive reason established through argument in the public sphere. The public sphere for Habermas is distinguished by an element of intersubjective communication, not mere association. Its political embodiment was first associated with the economic and political developments of the bourgeois era. (See the discussion of the public sphere in chapter 2.)

What Habermas seeks to overcome is the degeneration of the preconditions that makes the democratic public sphere possible. Instrumental rationality is the deforming element in modern discourse, and, as such, its
related institutions. The resultant distortions of intersubjective discourse—the type of discourse that characterizes the public sphere—
constitutes for Habermas the "colonization of the lifeworld" and "cultural
impoverishment."[12]

This colonization is as much a product of modernity as the public
sphere. In his book *Theory of Communicative Action,* Habermas claims
that the structures of intersubjectivity are implicit in the understanding
achieved in ongoing linguistic interaction and communicative action.
Communicative rationality—the type of rationality that arises from the
apodictic realization of the subject for the necessary precondition of (public) discourse for social interaction—guides practice and thus, for Habermas, functions as a criterion for political judgment.

For Habermas to secure a basis for normative judgments in a political
sense, he creates a system that suggests that current institutional forms of
discourse are salvageable through the reassertion of a capacity for linguistic competence. The competence of speakers and the political preconditions necessary for speakers to enact communicative reason serve as a
groundwork for practical political reason.

Beck and Offe inherit Habermas's concern with reflexivity as a necessity for democratic life. Indeed, each asserts that developments in the
economy, technology, and the state have simultaneously undermined reflexivity and generated new possibilities for its re-emergence. For both
Beck and Offe, the public sphere, as the location of reflexivity, is discovered in forms that remain outside the orbit of the state. Beck and
Offe, each in his own way, expand on Habermas's concerns: For each,
new social movement forms are structurally embedded in the same
processes that undermine reflexive abilities and accountability. Specifically, NSMs emerge in the nexus of the bureaucratic welfare state (Offe)
or in response to systemically produced hazards or risks administered
outside of public control (Beck). Traditional organs of contestational
politics, such as labor movements and parties, no longer retain critical
distance from the state and technology, and thus lose legitimacy and
cease to serve a democratizing function. NSMs represent the emergence
of spheres where collective actors support reflexivity or democracy in
nontraditional modes. Ulrich Beck calls this phenomenon "democratiza-
tion as the disempowerment of politics."[13]

Claus Offe sees NSMs as an historical phenomenon growing out of the contradictions (antagonisms) of modernizing capitalist societies. His assertion that NSMs largely comprise segments of a new middle class marked by a contradictory class location is shared by many others in the field.[14] According to the New Modernity theorists, national regulated markets of organized capitalism are being broken down by changes in the global market and international production. The effect is that the old class delineations no longer hold within the traditional nation–state. Furthermore, it is assumed that labor movements are in decline as are class-based voting blocks. In labor's place, NSMs have emerged as an expression of the growing numbers and influence of the middle class—in particular, some claim, its public sector professional employees. The new middle class, simultaneously dependent on the welfare state for income, yet defined by the increased production and dissemination of postmodern forms of culture, become both the consumers and producers of new cultural forms.[15] As is argued elsewhere,[16] the case that NSMs are an expression of the new middle class is less straightforward than it first appears, since NSM participants represent only a fraction of the overall middle class. Participants, after more detailed analysis, are identified both in terms of their structural emergence within post–WWII growth and related increases in education levels, *as well as* their relatively lower levels of privilege, income, and power within a differentiated new middle class. Additionally, NSMs include elements of what Offe terms peripheral or decommodified groups—those not socially defined by the labor market who also have flexible time schedules, such as middle-class homemakers, high school and university students, retirees, and marginally employed young people.[17] The New Modernity theorists of NSMs seem to suggest that these sectors of the middle class are concerned with noneconomic issues (i.e., ecology), which oppose further modernization in its classical industrial formulation. In general, NSMs, they argue, are concerned with issues of personal autonomy and identity (i.e., gender relations, ethnic identity, sexual preferences, etc.). As such, Beck and Offe argue that NSMs seek to reconstitute civil society away from the encroaching state and technology. This is accomplished by prefiguring alternative social arrangements, but through demands formulated, paradoxically enough, through constitutional rights arguments.[18] In both cases, old values receive new treatment.

In this perspective the general argument is that the Keynesian welfare state, in combination with increased technology, has broadened its social control capabilities and eroded the historical public sphere. Beck suggests that the once-liberating forces of the modern state and technology have generated conditions and risks, which simultaneously undermine and inspire reflexivity; reflexivity can be defined here as freedom of expression and nonconformism with dominant modes of rationality. The expanded state generates a new sense of entitlement, increases expectations, and, according to Beck, has achieved near-universal income security. At the same time, technology and science produce global "risks" that the state cannot "control." Parliamentarian or institutional politics lose their legitimacy, giving way to a new realm of subpolitics. Global threats posed by technology to individual rights and even survival depoliticize citizens away from the state and into spheres concerned with protecting autonomy. Beck, concerned with guaranteeing the continuation of rational discourse, suggests that this trend represents the continuation of modernity and not a negative moment. He argues:

Just as modernization dissolved the structure of feudal society in the nineteenth century, and produced the industrial society, modernization today is dissolving industrial society and another modernity is coming into being . . . the counter-modernistic scenario currently upsetting the world—new social movements and criticism of science technology and progress—does not stand in contradiction of modernity, but is rather an expression of reflexive modernity.[19]

Both Beck and Offe argue that NSMs emerge in the context of a globalized, high-tech economy, and national political structures characterized by neocorporatism. NSMs' adoption of noninstitutional politics has contributed to a view in which NSMs are seen as positing an alternative basis for politics in which radical transformation is neither predicated on class interest nor on formal institutional strategies. The lack of state orientation among NSMs, as well as their middle-class composition, are perceived to underpin a new politics that seeks to reconstitute civil society away from the state and the market by adopting practices that belong to an intermediate sphere between "private" pursuits and concerns on the one side, and institutional, state-sanctioned modes of politics on the other.[20] Success, in these terms, is defined *in opposition to* traditional representative institutions and relies heavily on the symbolic or rhetorical quality of the demand. Civil society, however, retains its more traditional "liberal" orientation.

The noneconomic demands and the noninstitutional orientation of NSMs are expressed in and through the decentralized organizational form and with an emphasis on direct democracy. Moving away from the traditional politics, NSMs, according to Offe, are fundamentally anti-statist. As prodigies of the expanded modern state, NSMs, the New Modernity theorists argue, hold a contradictory location that is further illustrated in their appropriation of modernist values (such as liberty and equality) to oppose further modernization. The combined effect of the structural expansion of the middle class within the political context of the bureaucratized state, it is argued, has produced NSMs that occupy ground that is neither economic nor formally political. The New Modernity theorists argue that NSM formations have enormous potential for challenging the "limitations, partial rigidities, instances of malfunctioning, and empirical evidence of deterioration"[21] of formal political institutions despite their "marginal, though highly visible position."[22] However, NSM theorists in general have spent little time applying their descriptions to actual movements.

When seen in the light of the outcomes of actual movements, it can be shown that all social movements, regardless of the era, are politically, ideologically, and economically constrained, and yet always retain the ideological ability to generate structural opportunities. This ability exists whether acknowledged or not. NSM theory fails to support this insight and instead contributes to its obfuscation. Social movements themselves, by way of interaction with the institutional and economic context, generate ideological repertoires that either reveal or submerge this same insight. In contrast, NSM theory attempts to structurally link specific ideological features to economic and bureaucratic trends. While institutional and economic tendencies and patterns exist, social movements are ultimately responsible for the interpretations and operations they assume within that context.

Beck and Offe each argue in various ways that NSM forms reflect a "new" reflexivity largely based on the assumption that the welfare state has secured a generalized middle class, or that risks generate reflexivity. In this regard, two aspects of the German political context may account for the degree of optimism inherent in such claims: the extent of the German welfare state and the range of strategic choices available to NSMs in a multi-party system. The relative degree of security afforded by the welfare state in Germany may indeed generate either greater numbers of NSM participants or a greater degree of confidence in their willingness to give up leisure time. Secondly, the success of the Greens in Germany, for example, cannot be appreciated outside of a set of electoral arrangements that accommodate minority views. Indeed, as I argue later, the "new" social movements in Europe depend on these two features for any measure of success. It is the lack of comparable *political and ideological* opportunity in the United States that retards American social movements. Indeed, NSMs, as expression of autonomy and identity claims, are poorly positioned to secure the institutional preconditions necessary for the realization of individual demands.

Yet, as discussed below, the concern with reconstituting the democratic elements of modernity, despite modernity's more negative or destructive consequences, distinguishes the New Modernity theorists from Post Modernity theorists in substantial ways. The New Modernity theorists' efforts to find continuity between contemporary social movement formations and those elements of the Enlightenment that stand for egalitarianism and justice speaks to a concern with theoretical coherence not evident in most of the Post Modernity theorists discussed below. Even though democratic ideals may be claimed by the Post Modernity theorists, there is little evidence in their formulations to suggest that they can justify such attachments. By embracing reason or reflexivity, the New Modernity theorists are admitting (and trying to justify) a normative criteria for political action aiming for the redemocratization of existing institutions. Despite their inability to institutionally secure such an attachment (a result of the subpolitical nature of NSMs), the concern at least concedes the need for guaranteeing rational communication in a democratic order. The Post Modernity theorists, while intending to be democratic, sidestep the issue altogether and are, ultimately, less coherent in their formulations.

THE POST MODERNITY THEORIES
OF NEW SOCIAL MOVEMENTS

The liberating force of modernity is exhausted as modernity triumphs.

Alain Touraine from *Critique of Modernity*

In their book, *Hegemony and Socialist Strategy*, Ernesto Laclau and Chantal Mouffe argue that the new multifarious forms of social conflict dissolve the privileged position Marxism gives the working class as an agent of social change. The theoretical crisis, as they describe it, spins off from this dissolution and points directly to the theoretical weaknesses of the old paradigm:

What is now in crisis is a whole conception of socialism which rests upon the ontological centrality of the working class, upon the role of Revolution, with a capital "r," as the founding moment in the transition from one type of society to another, and upon the illusory prospect of a perfectly unitary and homogeneous collective will that will render pointless the moment of politics. The plural and multifarious character of contemporary social struggles has finally dissolved the last foundations for that political imaginary. Peopled with "universal" subjects and conceptually built around History in the singular, it has postulated "society" as an intelligible structure that could be intellectually mastered on the basis of certain class positions and reconstituted, as rational, transparent order, through a founding act of political character. Today, the Left is witnessing the final act of the dissolution of that Jacobin imaginary.[23]

Laclau and Mouffe characterize the theoretical choices before contemporary social justice advocates as either Jacobin imaginary or articulatory practice, which consists of "the construction of nodal points which partially fix meaning."[24] Their view of Marxism associates the failures, including the totalitarian practices of Stalin, with the fixity and "rationalism of classical Marxism, which presented history and society as intelligible totalities constituted around conceptually explicable laws."[25] In this regard, Laclau and Mouffe are not only rejecting the teleological unity of Marxist theory along with the associated structural emergence of the working class, but they are also rejecting all generalized references to the accumulation process which, historically, presented a groundwork for unified struggle. In a certain way, Laclau and Mouffe mistakenly suggest that the oppressive politics of communist regimes is a direct result of not only the discredited teleological claims of Marxist theory but of rationalism in general. Their alternative approach rejects assumptions that link the social world to determinant economic structures, laws, or processes. In an all-or-nothing fashion, the alternative presented is a totally fluid social world somehow capable of transforming dominant relations into a radical and plural democracy founded on an "affirmation of the contingency and ambiguity of every 'essence' and on the constitutive character of social division and antagonism."[26] Their argument operates on a callow assumption that our paradigmatic choices are limited to Leninism and NSMs. The resultant indeterminacy of their positions unintentionally serves to rationalize an already fragmented social world, as well as divided, marginalized movements. Additionally, their position undercuts the potential crystallization of NSMs into truly counter-hegemonic forces because there is no persuasive reason to constitute themselves as units of power. By suggesting that economic, institutional, and ideological forces are, in a sense, beyond generalizable description, the postmodern approach of Laclau and Mouffe is not capable of stipulating the preconditions necessary for the democracy they desire. Unable to distinguish between these spheres of influence, NSMs are assigned "partially fixed meaning" in relation to the equally ambiguous forces that circumscribe reality. Indeterminacy, it follows, falsely ascribes NSMs a seemingly unrestrained ability to generate "nodal points" without concrete reference to institutional limits and restraints. The question then arises, from a pragmatic point of view, as to whether there exists a different set of theoretical and practical choices for social justice participants other than an overly determinant orthodox Marxism and an overly indeterminate cultural theory of radical politics.

Both Alberto Melucci and Alain Touraine also respond to the insufficiency of the old Marxist paradigm even while claiming connection to the concerns of the Frankfurt School in explaining current social movement trends. Unlike the New Modernity theorists, however, Melucci and Touraine attempt a reformulation of the class-centered account of mass movement formation by abandoning heuristic distinctions between the economy, formal institutions, and ideological forces. At the outset, each defines structures in more determinant ways than Laclau and Mouffe; however, like Laclau and Mouffe, they shed Enlightenment concepts evident in the New Modernity theorists by de-emphasizing reason and embracing the symbolic quality of movements. Melucci and Touraine, in shifting the locus of social movement action to the cultural realm, deny social movements any institutional or normative referent for judgment making. Each, in different ways, expresses concern that an adequate social movement theory must avoid stripping actors of the ability to give meaning to their actions, yet theory must also avoid ascribing NSMs the ability to create meaning without constraint. The shared presumption of a symbolic postindustrial world negates the ability to consider constraints in any strategic sense other than merely symbolic.

Melucci and Touraine present accounts of social movements in which contemporary struggles are affected by a shift in economic production from an industrial to a postindustrial system. This shift signifies a new era in which information, not wealth, becomes the basis for power. Resultant social conflicts differ from labor conflicts, in both contestation and goals. The major conflicts in society are no longer political or economic as were those of the industrial era. One observer states, "Instead of the predominantly economic orientations of the labor movement, contemporary struggles center around the spread of 'technocratic power' into all of social life, and democratic attempts to resist this control and formulate alternative paths of development."[27] Indeed, huge information controls induced by the state bureaucracies and corporate entities have made the struggle for *autonomy* of central concern. Postindustrial society has shifted modern social movements from political and economic terrain to sociocultural terrain. For both Melucci and Touraine, their accounts of the changes in the economy suggest the integration of previously semiautonomous spheres.

NSMs are engaged in struggles for autonomy in cultural—not political or economic—terms. Instead, their function is symbolic and self-referential. Melucci contends:

> The research findings in contemporary movements indicate the self-referential nature of their organizational forms. The organizational forms of movements are not just "instrumental" for their goals, they are goals in themselves. Since collective action is focused on cultural codes, the form of the movement is itself the message, a symbolic challenge to the dominant codes. Short-term and reversible commitment, multiple leadership, temporary and ad-hoc organizational structures are the basis for internal solidarity, but also for a symbolic confrontation with the external system. This confrontation signals the possibility of alternative experiences of time, space, and interpersonal relationships, which in turn challenge the technological rationality of the system.[28]

The reduction of political struggles to symbolic efforts to wrest meaning from technocratic controls assumes the irrelevance of political and economic demands apart from the amorphous demands of autonomy. Here the connection to reflexivity and reason that sustained a bridge between the old modernity and the new modernity for the theorists discussed above is no longer operative. Now NSMs are divorced not only from referential institutions, but from any rational criteria for decision making as well.

Alain Touraine's theory of social movements aims to locate the emancipatory sectors in society without relying on historically determinist explanations. Touraine's notion of postindustrial society is based on his 1969 claim that production had moved from a manufacturing base to an information base and that, as a result, the major social conflicts occur not between workers and owners, but between those with information and those without. For Touraine, information is embodied in the technocratic state: those without information are the public. The technocratic state, an integrated form of governing institutions and economic processes, is defined by bureaucratic rationality. Having institutionalized the social conflicts of the industrial era by absorbing the labor movement into parties, unions, and corporate arrangements, the technocratic state witnesses conflicts that are less concerned with reforming political institutions, and more concerned with creating and preserving a realm immune to technocratic domination.

NSMs are, in Touraine's view, the vehicles for resistance to institutionalization. For Touraine, a cycle of institutionalization and resistance characterizes history. For Touraine, resistance refers only to the "conflicts around the social control of the main cultural patterns."[29] Epochal characterizations like industrialism or postindustrialism determine the cultural pattern being contested. Technocratic life, then, becomes the core cultural pattern, which NSMs contest.

Critics argue, however, that while Touraine seeks to avoid the functionalism of RMT and the structural determinism associated with Marxism, his goal is undermined by his "adherence to a teleological periodization of societies, and by his insistence that we can identify a single social force in the form of a social movement, ideally suited to an oppositional role within 'postindustrial' society."[30] But these theoretical elements also present a practical concern: As movements unconcerned with issues of state power, how can the impact of NSMs on the technocratic culture be gauged? How is it that institutionalization occurs?

It is my argument that NSMs as defined by Touraine are assigned to a realm in which their contestational character can only be symbolic. As such, their impact is severely restricted when considered in light of the resources of the state or global corporations. Institutionalization, for Touraine, is tantamount to integration, so NSMs are faced with the choice of either absorption under the technocratic state or marginalization (at best). By submitting political, economic, and cultural institutions to one core cultural conflict, many possible strategic (political) and ideological choices are rejected a priori.

Alberto Melucci yields a similar result from a different approach. Melucci suggests a shift in social movement activity from the political and economic realm to the cultural. He is extremely clear in his assessment that "collective action is shifting more and more from the 'political' form, which was common to traditional oppositional movements in Western societies, to a cultural ground."[31] He argues:

> Postindustrial societies no longer have an "economic" basis; they produce by an increasing integration of economic, political, and cultural structures.

"Material" goods are produced and consumed with the mediation of huge informational and symbolic systems. Social conflicts move from the traditional economic/industrial system to cultural grounds: they affect personal identity, the time and space of everyday life, the motivations and cultural patterns of individual action. Conflicts reveal a major shift in the structure of complex systems, and new contradictions appear affecting their fundamental logic.[32]

Melucci makes these claims based on his observation of social movements of the 1980s in which he identifies actors who periodically and temporarily resist the pressure to conform to the informational and symbolic systems. Looking at movements such as the peace and disarmament movements of the eighties, Melucci proposes that they reveal "the transnational nature of contemporary problems and conflicts and the global interdependence of the planetary system."[33] He argues that to focus on the relationship between the movements and the political system, in particular the exhausted concept of the "nation-state," is to miss the most important function of NSMs. He says, "Collective action is not carried out simply for exchanging goods in the political market or for improving the participation in the system. It challenges the logic governing production and appropriation of social resources. They have a growing symbolic function."[34]

Melucci argues that NSMs offer a new organizational form that is far more than an instrumental vehicle for their goals. Described as temporary ad-hoc structures with rotating leadership that require sporadic commitment, he suggests that NSMs raise organization to the level of message in that the form itself prefigures. The existence of these forms alone challenge the dominant codes for Melucci, and thus old measures of movement success or failure miss the impact of NSMs.

It is important that all NSM theorists distinguish how it is that they thematize the relations between economic, political, and cultural/ideological forces and what relation this has on the strategies, forms, and demands they associate with NSMs. It is my contention that NSM theorists of both types resign NSMs to an ineffective sphere of activity based on certain erroneous assumptions about the relations between the economy, political institutions, and culture and ideology. As mentioned above, the New Modernity theorists deploy structural and economic accounts to assign NSMs to the cultural realm. This move overemphasizes the role of the economy in accounting for the emergence of NSM formations, while it strips NSMs of either economic or explicitly political interest. In my view, this is an attempt to give structural credence to the "highly informal, ad hoc, discontinuous, context-sensitive, egalitarian modes"[35] of NSMs on the mistaken, and perhaps sentimental, grounds that powerful mass movements have a structural base. New Modernity theorists attempt to give coherence to this formulation by merely asserting a connection between the new forms and rational reflection.

Likewise, the Post Modernity theorists, for different reasons, attempt to read NSMs in an enthusiastic manner, as evidence of new forms of resistance. In this case too, the forms and ideologies of NSMs are taken as confirmation of the irrelevance of economic and political modes in the new "postindustrial" world where traditional distinctions between the economy, political institutions, and culture and ideology are equally irrelevant. But, the experience of NSMs here in the United States indicates far less impact than either brand of NSM theorists suggest. In the United States, NSMs have a particularly hard time sustaining themselves as radical challenges in the midst of a two-party system, interest-group liberalism, and narrow ideological repertoires. It is my contention that such difficulty is fundamentally political, and, as such, contradicts the causal explanation of both types of NSM theory. In addition, the position and ascribed meanings given current social movements by NSM theorists also is misleading.

In the case of the New Modernity theorists, the production process and technology retain a structural link to the ideological features of social movements reminiscent of Marx. For the Post Modernists, system integration "produces" movements, but the economy or the state cease to function in the sense of generating particular interests. In each, the economy is not conceived as contributing to class interests based on economic disparities. Those class interests which, I argue, receive political, institutional, and ideological embodiment are perceived as irrelevant or nonexistent. In other words, class is not thought of as a set of *political* interests, but as a structural location or as synonymous with bureaucratization. Additionally, political institutions, conditioned by economic and ideological forces, receive no separate status in explaining the emergence of NSM demands.

Political institutions, equated with the over-reaching Keynesian welfare state or the technocratic state, are not considered arenas to be occupied or engaged by NSMs. Indeed, their structural assignment "elsewhere" prohibits NSMs from functioning in any other capacity except symbolic. It is my contention that the institutional and ideological forces in society, as expressive of class interests, generate and circumscribe NSM activity. NSM forms, I contend, are the conditioned responses—reflections—of dominant arrangements, which have discouraged self-understanding on the part of NSMs. While bureaucratic and economic centralization galvanizes itself, political controls weaken and disperse. NSM theory valorizes NSMs for this diffusion and reads this phenomena as indicative of a contestational alternative. It is my contention that NSMs are not in fact wholly "new" or necessarily contestational but, like traditional social movements, are essentially political and ideological phenomena conditioned by a systemic context that includes economic and political constraints to be contested. In this sense, NSMs are not unlike labor movements of the nineteenth and early twentieth centuries except that they lack a persuasive ideology that relates the three spheres (economy, ideology, and institutions) in a coherent set of demands and strategy. As such, to achieve the autonomy and rights demanded, they must engage in attempts at a new self-understanding that grasps current economic, political, and ideological conditions.

NEW SOCIAL MOVEMENTS AND POWER

At the same time, NSM theory raises a set of concerns that neither RMT nor the old Marxist paradigm are capable of accommodating. Carl Boggs, in his book *Social Movements and Political Power,* raises a series of questions concerning the relationship between NSMs and the international economy as well as the nation–state, which acknowledges the contributions of NSM theory while considering its problems. Boggs begins with the acknowledgment that the forms identified do indeed exist in some measure as described. While Boggs raises the strategic deficiencies associated with NSMs in both these contexts, he also posits their emergence as significant.

For Boggs, NSMs indicate "the necessity of multiple paradigms in a situation where the prospects for a single unifying agency (social or political) have vanished." NSMs, he argues, indicate the need for "a critical dialectical framework that contains a philosophy of praxis that is no longer wedded to the canons of scientific materialism or to the primacy of objective historical forces; a social theory that confronts the reality of multiple and overlapping forms of domination without reducing that reality to one of its aspects."[36] For Boggs, despite the strategic inadequacies, NSMs

provoke needed theoretical innovation. The old Marxist categories are, for
Boggs, inadequate in that they "present the image of a bipolar world characterized by epochal struggle between two competing world–historical
forces—wage labor and capital, proletariat and bourgeoisie, socialism and
capitalism."[37] Yet, it remains unclear here how NSMs are to conceive of
the accumulation process (as well as the state) and how they are to amend
the deficiencies he points up.

Boggs' concerns seem to be twofold: that Marxism is incompatible
with contemporary social movement reality and that the search for
global laws of social development tied to an historical logic are out-
worn and deadening for contemporary social justice movements. Boggs
is legitimately critical of the scientific unity attributed to history within
Marxism. At the same time, it is extremely important to note that Boggs
does not valorize the disunity among NSMs that I argue is enshrined in
much of the theory. Like Offe, Boggs suggests that alliances or greater
unity among NSMs may increase their effect, yet neither theorist can
resolve the insufficiency of NSMs' impact, or their lack of success in
creating alliances, given the theoretical justifications they offer for
NSMs' existence. The two propositions (the structural creation of discontinuous forms and a political interest in unity and coherence) are
contradictory. Despite the fact that the Marxist teleology is no longer
tenable, the outline of a "post" Marxist theory based on NSMs remains
vague. Unlike the Post Modernists, Boggs seems to worry that NSMs
have problems grasping the mediating elements of social, political, and
economic power. The problem of reconciling immanence and trans-
cendence continues to have meaning for Boggs despite the fact that an
alternative scheme, which suggests the possibility for overcoming
economic, political, and ideological obstacles to democratic rule, remains ambiguous in both the New Modernity theorists and the Post
Modernists.

For Boggs, as well as for Post Modernists like Laclau and Mouffe,[38]
the concept of hegemony, as developed by Antonio Gramsci, is forwarded as a basis for reformulating the determinism of historical materialism. Hegemony, it is hoped, will assist in thematizing the relations
between economic, political, and ideological forces and the rise and
outcomes of NSMs in a way that explains both NSM origins, yet avoids
teleological closure. This appears to be an attempt to preserve a structural basis for mass movements for social change, and at the same time
account for what is perceived to be the noneconomic interests of cur-

rent social movements. Hegemony is one such strategy. Yet, the concept as reformulated offers little clarification of the dilemmas facing NSMs in the United States.

Various NSM theorists interpret Gramsci's work in such a way that counter-hegemonic institutions come to mean a type of diffuse social movement instead of an opposition party capable of assuming state power (as Gramsci originally intended). As a result, NSMs lack strategies that actually contest state or economic power in any determinate way. As Bobbio has argued, Gramsci made two contributions to Marxist theory: He emphasized the primacy of the ideological realm (superstructure) over the economic structure in determining revolutionary consciousness, and he considered both civil society and the state to be elements of the superstructure. In Gramsci, civil society and the state become two levels of the superstructure: two moments—one private and one political—through which the dominant group exercises command and through which that command may be challenged. This formulation in Gramsci gives the socialist struggle a fundamentally ideological character, which is why he is so appealing to NSM theorists. It seems to me an entirely different claim and foreign to Gramsci, however, to see this as conflating economic and state functions and processes. The reason Gramsci developed the concept of hegemony was that it enabled him to explain the lack of a socialist revolution despite ripe "objective conditions."

This lack of teleological closure indicated to Gramsci that economism cannot explain the rise and fall of movements. Instead, parties were seen as essential for success due to the fact that they were conceived as ideological spaces and political organizations directed *both* toward state activity *and* its transformation. However, by celebrating the new forms (over and against parties), both New Modernity and Post Modernity theorists of NSMs have emphasized the cultural aspects in lieu of political power. Ultimately, they reject the relevance of parties (as ends in themselves and in how they impact social movement outcomes) and have enshrined the symbolic character of NSMs. In response to various forms of economism and fatalism, NSM theorists claiming a connection to Gramsci are struggling with the indeterminate character of social movements today. Unfortunately, the rejection of participatory state-oriented strategies, and the construing of the economy in an undifferentiated manner (rather than seeing the economy as generating class interests that require ideological understanding), has made it difficult to resolve the gap between NSM aspirations and outcomes. The problems with NSM theory really come into view when dealing with NSMs in the United States. In the American context, where state and institutional politics are limited and designed to discourage institutional access in the first place, and dominant ideology functions to restrain NSMs from considering the obstacles to their effectiveness, the gap between aspirations and outcomes is enormous.

The reconceptualization of hegemony in Boggs jettisons Gramsci's notion of a party. In an attempt to celebrate the new, the theoretical move from parties to localized, fragmented groupings appears to be an uncritical acceptance of the new forms of organizing. In essence, this move demonstrates the fundamental contradiction of the New Modernity theorists as well: The assumption that systemic forces continue to function as a basis for social movement formation contradicts their rejection of either the teleology or the functional determinism associated with Marxism. Instead, New and Post Modernity theorists retain systemic accounts of movement origins but reroute the link directly to noninstitutional arenas, bypassing politics at both junctures. Ironically, New Modernity and Post Modernity theorists end up preserving some of the least useful elements of the old Marxist paradigm and inventing new connections that simply ascribe outcomes to NSMs that are empirically not evident.

Developing an approach that thematizes both systemic and contingent (political) aspects of NSMs in our era is no small task. But certainly any such effort that suggests that politics traditionally conceived is irrelevant to the transformative potential of NSMs will, in the end, be hamstrung by its own assumptions. New social movements, I will argue in the next chapter, are not only dependent on the political guarantees of the modern liberal state, but will greatly benefit from seeing themselves in relation to the besieged norms and processes evident in a type of *reason* that is both brought about and threatened by modernizing forces.

NOTES

1. *The Village Voice,* July 20, 1993, pp. 28–32.

2. Claus Offe, "New Social Movements: Challenging the Boundaries of Institutional Politics," *Social Research,* vol. 52, n. 4 (Winter 1985), p. 829.

3. Jean Cohen, "Strategy or Identity: New Theoretical Paradigms and Contemporary Social Movements," *Social Research,* vol. 52, n. 4 (Winter 1985), p. 664.

4. For a representative and in many respects foundational view, see "Resource Mobilization and Social Movements: A Partial Theory" by John McCarthy and Mayer Zald, *American Journal of Sociology,* vol. 82 (1977).

5. Enrique Larana, Hank Johnston, and Joseph R. Gusfield, eds., *New Social Movements: From Ideology to Identity* (Philadelphia: Temple University Press, 1994), "Introduction," p. 5.

6. This assumes the political–economic context in which the NSMs are said to arise.

7. These efforts are well represented in the work by Doug McAdam (i.e., "Culture and Social Movements") and many others appearing in Larana, Johnston, and Gusfield's edited collection, *New Social Movements*. Other contributions, from both sides of the fence, are evident in the collection *Cultural Politics and Social Movements*, edited by Marcy Darnovsky, Barbara Epstein, and Richard Flacks (Philadelphia: Temple University Press, 1995).

8. See *From Mobilization to Revolution* (Reading, Mass.: Addison Wesley, 1978). For an excellent introduction to his extended argument in *The Contentious French* (Cambridge: Belknap Press, 1986), see "Models and Realities of Popular Collective Action," in *Social Research*, vol. 52, n. 4 (1985).

9. My arguments regarding the importance of the state for new social movement impact relies heavily on the assumption that the accumulation process, as a force that significantly undermines democratic potential, cannot be even minimally muted without reliance on the state's legislative and welfare functions and the reform of electoral arrangements.

10. Jurgen Habermas, "Tasks of a Critical Social Theory" in *Jurgen Habermas on Society and Politics,* edited by Stephen Seidman (Boston: Beacon Press, 1989), p. 93.

11. See Offe's discussion of potential alliances beginning on p. 856 of his above-cited article.

12. See Jurgen Habermas, *Philosophical Discourse of Modernity,* trans. by Frederick Lawrence (Cambridge: MIT Press, 1987).

13. Ulrich Beck, *The Risk Society: Towards a New Modernity* (London: Sage Publications, 1992), p. 191.

14. See Gunnar Oloffson, "After the Working-Class Movement? An Essay on What's 'New' and What's 'Social' in the New Social Movements," in *Acta Sociologica,* vol. 31 (1988).

15. For a provocative discussion of the middle class thesis, see Paul Bagguley's review article "Social Change, the Middle Class and the Emergence of New Social Movements: A Critical Analysis," in *Sociological Review,* vol. 40 (1992).

16. See Oloffson (and discussed in Alan Scott's book *Social Movements and Ideology*).

17. Offe (1985), p. 834.

18. See Beck, chapter eight "Opening Up the Political" in *Risk Society*.

19. Beck, pp. 10–11.

20. Offe, p. 820.

21. Offe, p. 854.

22. Offe, p. 857.

23. Ernesto Laclau and Chantal Mouffe, *Hegemony and Socialist Strategy* (London: Verso Press, 1985), p. 2.

24. Laclau and Mouffe, p. 113.

25. Laclau and Mouffe, p. 3.

26. Laclau and Mouffe, p. 193.

27. Kenneth Tucker, "Ideology and Social Movements: The Contributions of Habermas," *Sociological Inquiry,* vol. 59, no.1 (1989), p. 36.

28. Alberto Melucci, *Nomads of the Present* (Philadelphia: Temple University Press 1989), p. 60.

29. Alain Touraine, "An Introduction to the Study of Social Movements," in *Social Research,* vol. 52, no. 4 (1985), p. 760.

30. Alan Scott, "Action, Movement, and Intervention: Reflections on the Sociology of Alan Touraine," in *Canadian Review of Sociology & Anthropology,* vol. 28 (1991), p. 31.

31. Alberto Melucci, "The Symbolic Challenge of Contemporary Movements," in *Social Research,* vol. 52, no. 4 (1985), p. 789.

32. Ibid. p. 746.

33. Ibid. p. 807.

34. Ibid. p. 797 and p. 798.

35. Offe (1985), p. 829.

36. Boggs, pp. 16–17.

37. Boggs, p. 57.

38. The difference between Boggs' and Laclau and Mouffe's appropriation of Gramsci is that Boggs, as closer to the new modernity theorists, retains a degree of autonomy for the economic sphere as did Gramsci, whereas Laclau and Mouffe borrow Gramsci's term despite the fact that they regard economic, political, and cultural forces as indistinguishable.

Chapter Two

Reason, Politics,
and Social Movements

On the road toward science, social philosophy has lost what politics
formerly was capable of providing as prudence.

Jurgen Habermas from *Theory and Practice*

Everywhere we look, conventional understandings of politics are in crisis.
From different perspectives, a shift seems to be pulling apart, wearing
down, reorganizing, or perhaps simply obliterating a notion of politics that
has been limping along since the Enlightenment. From the effects of globalization on the legitimacy of the traditional state to the participation
crises evidenced by the decline in voting and party identification, the al-
ready-dirty word "politics" has gotten even dirtier. If, for purposes here,
we conceive of the political as those matters relating to the governing
institutions—including the norms, processes, and means of legitimation—
of liberal representative democracy, then it becomes clear that enthusiasm
for politics among the general population has become a dot in the rear-
view mirror of history.

At the same time, grievances abound. Complaints, anomie, pathologies
(both physiological and psychological in nature), and hardships relating to
survival permeate social life. What citizens experience on the personal
level—and here I have most in mind the American version—appears unconnected to, or at least unresolvable by the state, by representatives, or
by constitutions. Despite the remnants of power that remain in those
corridors, there is a pervasive sense that whatever is steering society, it
is not politics. Of course, collective action surfaces. But, as new social

movement (NSM) theorists argue, what makes much of it new is its orientation to the social and its disinterest in resuscitating traditional political forms.

At the same time, much of social theory is in retreat from politics as well. In various guises, the traditional idea of governing institutions as legitimate arenas for the resolution of social and political grievances has become passé. In its more severe philosophical form, this attitude expresses itself in the radical skepticism of postmodernism, which, despite debate over a generalizable meaning for the term, rejects the possibility of thematizing social reality concretely.[1] In a different vein, much in contemporary social theory equates politics with bureaucratic and instrumental rationality and conflates the effects (and roles) of the state and the economy on social life.[2] Along with the descriptions of the subsumption of political ideals under the demands of technological and economic interests is an accompanying pessimism or indifference as to the value of retrieving institutions associated with these ideals. Often positioned against these homogenizing effects are the phenomena dubbed "new" social movements. The traditional state (i.e., the liberal welfare state)—against and away from which the NSMs are conceived—is thematized out of the picture. Generally speaking, the opposition to politics, which the NSMs have come to symbolize, has become a predominant feature of social theory.

With increasing academic intensity, the study of social movements has become something of a boom industry in the last ten years. In many respects this is an encouraging surprise. After all, it was just a decade or so ago that giddy pronouncements of the triumph of liberalism fell on the uneasy ears of social critics.[3] At the same time, popular philosophical trends seemed to contest all forms of intersubjective communication and therefore unified resistance to arbitrary power. In actual fact, the 1980s and much of the 1990s witnessed widespread resistance to conservative governments and such seemingly diverse policies as constructive engagement with South African apartheid, restrictions on women's reproductive rights, deregulation of environmental protection, deprioritizing of the AIDS crisis, unilateral and often covert U.S. interventions (i.e., Iran, Grenada, Panama, Libya, Nicaragua, and El Salvador), assaults on social spending of all types, the reassertion of patriarchal family values, nuclear power development, and university deliberalization, among others. Intellectuals interested in prospects for the progressive transformation of the status quo turned to social movements for inspiration. Of course, this makes sense in many respects: The social movements appearing in advanced capitalist nations since the 1960s have indeed signaled a definitive shift away from status quo politics and have often been the bearers, however symbolically, of demands for increased liberty, freedom, justice, and egalitarian forms. At the same time, the divorce of social and political grievances from state channels of expression has not—as much of the NSM theory suggests, automatically signaled a rise in demands for justice or freedom. Indeed, nothing short of an outpouring of reporting and scholarship on right-wing social movements has appeared since the Oklahoma City bombing in 1995, the numerical and political growth of the Christian right throughout the nineties, and the persistent expansion of neofascist movements in Europe over the last ten years.[4] Interestingly enough, to a point the rise of right-wing social movements can be explained using the same theories that seek to explain their more left-leaning counterparts. But the self-understandings of social movements, including their posture toward formal institutions, are crucial in gauging their character and influence. Among the characteristics that sets the two types apart is the fact that right-wing social movements are, however cynically, willing to operate at the level of politics in ways that their left-wing counterparts are not. As a result, right-wing social movements, like the U.S. Christian Coalition, revive and redirect traditional politics while gaining influence over new modes.

It has become increasingly apparent that whatever large-scale trends we might identify to help explain the emergence of "new" social movements, these structural or systemic explanations alone will not account for the normative orientation and political impact of the disparate movements. Indeed, the self-directed action of social movements demands an approach that can combine systemic explanations of what makes their potential emergence possible in the first place, along with normative assessments that privilege the political context, choices, and consequences endemic to social movement aims and forms. This project, I contend, necessarily follows in the tradition of critical social theory, with its critical insights into the accumulation process and, owing to Habermas, the understanding of the need to develop social practices that emphasize reason as a communicative process. In that sense, and as Habermas's work on both the public sphere and, more recently, on modern law demonstrates,[5] such an approach must eventually rely on political concerns. In other words, far from conceding the political, I contend that there exist practical, systemically related imperatives that require social movements and social theorists to focus on securing besieged norms through political institutions, however provisionally.

Practical realities demand a reassertion of political criteria (the proposing of binding norms and their institutional counterparts) so that a more
distinguishing explanation of social movements and social transformation
might develop. But much more than this is at stake. Beyond clarifying explanations, the actual preconditions for the kind of critical discursive practice that liberal representative democracy—and its reform—assumes must
either be vigorously reasserted at the level of institutions, or be lost between the seemingly paradoxical pressures of, on the one hand, strategic
parochial interests like the Christian Right and, on the other, global high-
tech capitalism with its renewed disregard for democracy and traditional
constitutional controls.[6]

The preconditions for defending against the further encroachment of the
potential for reform include the preservation of the rule of law in conjunction with the expansion of consonant "public sphere"[7] institutions
such as democratic social movements and parties. More specifically, social movements and parties, as mechanisms of political control and public accountability, must be willing to call into question the institutional
and economic obstacles to a more accessible and viable public sphere. The
institutional suspension of economic and other resource hindrances must
be asserted against the mounting pressures of daily life. In this sense, the
further specification of what makes a social movement emancipatory in
character ends up relying on how that movement stands in relation to such
preconditions.

It is not enough to simply suggest that social movements qua social
movements move against the tide of "homogenization." In this sense, developing criteria that allow a distinction between emancipatory v. regres-
sive social movement trends requires privileging political norms and thematizing their institutional expression. This effort both requires and
furthers an increased reflexivity about the current conditions of modernity
that can only be controlled through political means. In this sense, social
movement theorists (and participants) will continue to be caught off
guard, empirically speaking, where they occlude the unavoidably political
character of the subject at hand.

Any effort of this kind will need to focus on the structural macro-
dynamics of society along with the interplay between such dynamics and
the self-understandings, projected aims, and actual impacts of social
movements. Understandably, perhaps, social movement analysis has really been the province of sociologists. And while sociology has made
enormous contributions to the study of social movements, the falsity of

separate disciplines reveals itself here when confronted with the sociopolitical character of movements. In many respects, sociology's core agenda has revolved around explaining the kinds of social shifts and eruptions that social movements embody. As Jurgen Habermas has suggested, "Sociology originated as a discipline responsible for the problems that politics and economics pushed to one side on their way to becoming specialized sciences."[8]

For Habermas, the task of reconstructing a critical social theory adequate to explain the rise of social movements (and evaluate their validity) shares its greatest affinity with the sociological tradition. Indeed, knowing Habermas's intense interest in the normative aspects of social and political life, this statement makes perfect sense given the sociological traditions of Europe. There, interpretive sociology and critical theory generally have gained greater acceptance for a longer period of time than in the United States. In comparison, the dominant sociological approaches in the United States, particularly when speaking of social movement studies, have emphasized decision-theoretic, strategic-action approaches—not approaches in which methodological assumptions are subjected to metatheoretic, normative critique.

Admittedly, as social science disciplines, both political science and sociology have evidenced parallel developments and phases, and each has fallen prey to types of functionalism and positivism that employed, in Horkheimer's critical sense of the term, degrees of "scientistism."[9] But just as sociology offers a critical approach, so too does the study of politics. Critical interpretation of traditional complexes of political meaning can be a fruitful way of gaining insight. The assumption here is that to the extent that Western political traditions have structured pragmatic understandings, it is worthwhile to interpret their possible applications to an otherwise normatively conceived project of emancipation. And for reasons I seek to demonstrate below, there may indeed be a historically significant contribution that can be honed out of the difference between the two disciplines. This contribution may lie in the emphasis that the discipline of politics places on the need for securing norms in formal political institutions. Taking heed not to diminish sociology's insight into the increasingly relevant arena of the "social" as a basis for reflection and action, it is by way of the tradition of political theory that the persistent problem of securing the institutional preconditions for reflexivity and action presents itself so persuasively against the contemporary problem of the subsumption of politics under modernization's calculus. Whether one is talking about reason, reflexivity, or communicative rationality, the institutional preconditions for its expression eventually press in on the theoretical act.

LIMPING ALONG: DEMOCRACY AND REASON

The efforts of political theorists for more than three centuries to guarantee political democracy through epistemologies, ontologies, or philosophies of history remind us, ironically, of the related yet contingent relationship between "reason" and democracy. The imperative for securing a capacity and criteria for judgment in the defense of representative democracy has given reason its prominent role. And, to borrow the old polemical phrase, this is no accident.

What is considered reason in much of modern Western political thought is a sometimes hedged desire for the guarantees of intersubjective communication, judgment, and agreement so necessary for democratic life. Often packed into the one concept of reason are the cognitive, normative, and procedural preconditions for democracy. Against monarchy and servitude, political theorists in the Enlightenment tradition have been trying to defend democracy by way of reference to reason. But as critical social theory has demonstrated, reason was never so unproblematic. Indeed, the institutions and processes of modernity assumed to house and foster reason have themselves been the brokers of an undermining instrumentalism wedded to efficiency and profits. The question remains whether the Enlightenment preoccupation with reason has anything to contribute to modernity's democratic dilemmas.

Before considering a contemporary reformulation of reason, it is worthwhile to investigate the various ways in which modern political theorists have sought to secure reason on the road to democracy. Two things are at stake in such an inquiry: the identification of the role purportedly played by reason and the view toward its institutionalization. In other words, while reason and democracy appear linked by way of philosophical foundations in the works of the authors considered below, contemporary readers can benefit from seeing these as normative arguments aiming for social and political institutionalization. In keeping with this perspective, the actual institutionalization of certain liberal norms linked to reason, however undermined by modernization, continue, I suggest, to structure pragmatic understandings. Their validity as both pragmatic and normative criteria serve as a potential basis for reform. In this sense, the architecture of modern political theory, both philosophical and institutional, reminds us of the value in excavating a notion of reason in defense of democracy and its reform.

These days, not many will argue with the assertion that the Enlightenment was not all that it was cracked up to be. Indeed, the legacy of the Enlightenment and its thinkers can be discovered in the odd transformation of many of its premises into their opposites. While science aimed to liberate humanity from mysticism and convention, it has instead brought about technological capacities for new servitude and even extinction. Modernity, as such, has brought with it practical consequences that demonstrate that the technological and economic forces set in motion since the seventeeth century have not been consonant with the political ideals professed. As if painfully aware of the tentative affinity between emancipation and the new scientific reason, political theorists in the liberal tradition demonstrate a near obsession with grounding democracy in the very same reason that seemed to be unleashed in science and the production processes.

Modernization, however, has proven their effort a fantasy. Quite to the contrary, the democratic practice desired could not be engineered by epistemological, ontological, historical, or even utilitarian schemes while considering reason under a single, undifferentiated meaning. Reason, as it was conceived in relation to democracy, was imbued with a normative content not borne out by its expression in other arenas of society.

Reason's relationship to liberalism and its reform is a varied one. What is most easily said about the relationship is that regardless of the philosophical tack, reason supplies political meaning. By reviewing three formulations of reason by liberal and reformist theorists, we can see how the persistent problem of securing governing norms repeatedly receives philosophical grounding schemes as a solution. As reason takes on differentiated and more instrumental forms with industrialization, philosophers' attachment to reason as a normative foundation for democracy pulls apart. The substance of reason's early formulations takes on an independent character that dangles despite efforts to recapture the perceived connection.

FROM CONTRACTS TO CONTEXT:
SOME GROUNDS FOR REASON

Whether we look to the first social contract theorist, Hobbes, or to the moral groundwork of Kant, or even to the contextual, pragmatic approach of Dewey, a relationship between the assumptions about reason and proposed political forms presents itself. And this is no less true given the very different versions of liberalism these thinkers proffer. Hobbes, Kant, and Dewey each represent a fundamentally different philosophical tack (ontological, epistemological, pragmatic) to the problem of reason. Toward explaining their differences, the course of political and technological events from the turn of the seventeenth to the turn of the nineteenth centuries offers some guidance. Still, as thinkers in the Enlightenment tradition, each struggles with a defense of self-controlling publics that requires the presence of reasoning subjects capable of agreeing on binding norms.

While these thinkers grapple with different historical phases of liberalism, they share three common concerns: an identification of reason, its role in establishing binding norms, and the development of the institutional preconditions for its exercise. In each case, the formulation of reason provides a link between the normative content of freedom in their work, and the social and political order. In each case, the need to secure norms and competencies becomes crucial to the defense of liberalism. And while reason does receive different treatments in these thinkers, its formulation can be seen to direct political forms. Indeed, for contemporary purposes, there are practical lessons to be found in examining and identifying these affinities. And despite the permanent rupture between fantasy and reality, between bourgeois idealism and the modernization processes, the practical importance of reason persists. This, I will argue later in this chapter, is poignantly illustrated in new social movements.

REASON AS MECHANICAL SELF-INTEREST

The work of Thomas Hobbes (1588–1679) is fundamentally influenced by the discoveries of science as well as the economic mobility and spiritual insecurity those discoveries helped usher in. As a social contract theorist, Hobbes derives political authority from individual action based in reason: The individual consents to the forgoing of unlimited liberty in the state of nature in exchange for the protection of the sovereign through the social contract. In *Leviathan*, Hobbes develops an explanation for how human beings come to understand and evaluate themselves, their environment, and their interests. Crucial to the explanation is Hobbes's application of a causal interpretation of natural science applied to human nature and human reasoning capacities. His conception of reason as a causal response aimed at maximizing self-interest underpins his politics. That is to say, Hobbes's recourse to the absolute control of the sovereign is a consequence of reason as a calculation of interests that cannot alone support "civil prudence." Order substitutes for rightness.

It is appropriate to echo C. B. MacPherson in his characterization of Hobbes's theory of human nature as a kind of mechanical materialism.[10] Using the "resolutive–compositive" method he appropriated from the geometry of his day, Hobbes set about in the first book of *Leviathan* to reduce man and society to a "mechanical system of matter in motion."[11] Hobbes posits that the sum total of man and society, including reason, can be deduced from certain laws of motion:

> The cause of sense is the External Body, or Object, which presseth the organ proper to each Sense, either immediately as in the Taste and Touch; or mediately, as in Seeing and Hearing, and Smelling: which pressure, by the mediation of Nerves, and other strings, and membranes of the body, continue inwards toward the Brain, and Heart, causeth there a resistance, or counter-pressure.[12]

Among the multitude of pressures in the world on the senses of man, Hobbes suggests that man himself is moved by appetites (motion toward) and aversions (motion away) along the same principles and in the same manner of objects. Out of the constant barrage of sensory impact, man must somehow organize the information in order to move and survive in the world. This is accomplished through the faculty reason.

Hobbes describes reason as a faculty of the mind, possessed by all men, that functions along the principles of addition and subtraction. His conception of reason is mechanistic and unencumbered by notions of human sentiment or morality. Together with his picture of man possessing an inherent drive for domination (motion toward) fueled by fear of death (motion away), reason serves only in summing or subtracting axiomatically determined ideas. Reason as nature supplies both the drive for maximizing individual interests and the need to establish limits on liberty when it threatens extinction. Reason, as such, lacks a moral quality to the extent that it is conceived entirely based on strategic self-interest. Reason in this sense becomes tied not to virtue, as it is in the classical tradition, but to the protection of pleasure as the free use and enjoyment of possessions. If reason supplied a moral quality, conflict would not be so prevalent and protection so needed. Reasoning leads to conflict, which eventually refers

individuals to the need for binding norms to preserve a degree of liberty
to pursue self-interest. Hobbes differentiates this insight from something
akin to truth:

> Not but that all Reason it self is always Right Reason, as well as Arith-
> metic is a certain and infallible Art: But no man's Reason, nor the Reason
> of any one number of men, makes the certainty; no more than an account
> is therefore well cast up, because a great many men have unanimously ap-
> proved it.[13]

Hobbes's Right Reason is not to be found by man in nature. The lack of
truth criteria in nature's reason will necessarily create dispute among men.
In Hobbes's state of nature, the inclination toward competition and conflict over goods already cast a situation of chaos. It is from this set of assumptions that Hobbes deduces the need for an ultimate judge, an un-
questioned arbiter. In the move from the state of nature to civil society, the
absolute sovereign now becomes reason's authority. The agreement to
submit to the absolute sovereign does not imply that in fact the sovereign
is possessed of more perfect deduction, only that he is bound by the social
contract to preserve the peace by any means necessary.

Hobbes's notion of reason as a mechanistic mental capacity does not
allow him to make any epistemological claim to reason as a normative
basis for judgment. His move to rule "by the sword" is a faithful, if not
nervous, response to the lack of truth criteria resulting from his view of
reason as physiologically induced calculation of self-interest.

REASON AS MORAL JUDGMENT

Immanuel Kant (1729–1797) began his project in the shadow of
Rousseau's General Will. Rousseau's formulation of the General Will un-
convincingly attempted to bridge the normative gap between Hobbesian
self-interest and the desire for a democratic and egalitarian society.
Rousseau's "Assembly of the People" presented for Kant a need to ground
a moral foundation for society in such a way that binding norms would
exist apart from the calculation of autonomous wills. At the same time,
Kant seeks to secure respect for the autonomy of the individual subject.
His intention was to minimize the opposition of private interest in such a
way that citizens' public conduct would be in keeping with universaliz-
able norms necessary for survival.

Kant was dissatisfied with the state-of-nature justifications of the social contract approach. Instead, Kant opted for a social contract with an epistemological grounding, which posits reason as the human capacity for moral judgment. Looking to the constitutional state to operate according to axiomatically derived imperatives, the democratic tallying of preferences takes a back seat. Kant successfully provides reason with a normative quality, links that quality to the operation of the state, but then hedges on the reliability of humans to employ their reason appropriately.

In *Groundwork for the Metaphysics of Morals*, Kant establishes a general or universal principle for civil society in quite a different manner than Rousseau or the other contract theorists before him. Kant begins by taking up the epistemological foundation for reason as the capacity for moral judgment. Like liberal theorists before him, Kant shares a concern with autonomy—not an autonomy of the will, but an autonomy that stands in relation to the subjective capacity shared by all humans. By positing transcendental categories of apperception, the subject that emerges is an "I" defined by self-reflection. This moral quality of reason is manifested by the human ability to reflect on one's actions in relation to others. This is a quality, Kant suggests, that humans must attribute to themselves to account for everyday moral consciousness.[14] In a sense, the practical demands for the resolution of conflict between self-interest and duty to others receives epistemological priority.

For Kant, this idea of reason as the shared capacity for moral judgment realizes itself as a political moment through the categorical imperative. Axiomatically derived from the shared capacity for moral judgment, the categorical imperative directs humans to see others as reasoning autonomous subjects and to treat them as ends in themselves. Moreover, the imperative, in Kant's words, directs that "I ought never to act except in such a way that I can also will that my maxim should become universal law."[15] Kant elaborates the civil function of the categorical imperative in his discussion of public right.

In *Metaphysics of Morals*, Kant makes clear that consent to laws need not be determined by summing the votes of the people. Instead, legitimacy may be gauged to the extent that the laws passed or judged are judged according to the categorical imperative. The form of government he advocates is not that of a direct democracy, but a republican form, even as mixed monarchy, in which the principle of universal law constitutes sovereignty. The formalizing of the rule of law apart from an accounting of individual subjects accounts for his de-emphasis of participation.

Kant's system posits the need for the formalization in law of a critical standard for judgment. Without a normative standard for judgment, Kant regards all human action and contemplation of what "ought" to be as incomprehensible. However, the drive to develop law grounded in an epistemologically conceived notion of moral reasoning ultimately results in political formalism detached from democratic practice. Without foundation in the everyday practices of reasoning subjects, their participation becomes superfluous to the proper functioning of the state.

REASON AS CONTEXTUAL INQUIRY

Democratic practice is the central philosophical concern of America's most famous representative of pragmatism, John Dewey (1860–1952). Writing in the first half of the twentieth century, Dewey saw modernity as both threatening and wonderful. It is a tension that defines his work, and as I argue later, occupies much of contemporary social theory.

Clearly continuing in the Enlightenment tradition, Dewey viewed both the method of scientific inquiry and democracy as prizes of modernity. Yet equally a part of modernity, he observed, was the stagnation and delocalization of life under the modern nation–state and international capitalism. Recapturing democratic practice for Dewey relies on citizens' use of a type of reason implied in every problematic situation in which resolution based on a consideration of consequences is sought. Eschewing epistemological formulations as "spectator theories of knowledge," Dewey seeks to unite reason and democracy by way of observable processes rooted in human association.

The central conflict of modern life for Dewey is the dissolving of previously cohesive communities. The breaking down of social bonds threatens the very idea of democracy:

> Changes in domestic, economic, and political relations have brought about a serious loosening of the social ties which hold people together in definite and readily recognizable relations. The machine, for example, has come between the worker and the employer; distant markets intervene between producer and consumer . . . in countless ways the customary loyalties that once held men together and made them aware of the reciprocal obligations have been sapped.[16]

Dewey's pragmatic proscriptions for overcoming the skewed nature of democracy in the modern age are outlined in his work *The Public and Its*

Problems. His efforts there are informed by three assumptions: all action, including thought, is necessarily context-dependent; associated or "co-joint" activity is an organic and necessary but insufficient condition for community, which is moral in character and consciously sustained; and the sustaining of a democratic public depends on an identifiable process of inquiry characterized by the observance and consideration of consequences. The emergence of democratic community out of mere association (including modern manifestations) is, therefore, dependent on the practice of inquiry.

Dewey's notion of inquiry, in accord with his opposition to traditional epistemological frameworks (Kant), is framed by his pragmatist's concern with the practical, the evident, the present. Likewise, his notion of inquiry must be consonant with his democratic ethic and must remain open-ended and changeable. To avoid the separation of norms and democratic participation that was evident in Kant, Dewey substitutes a "pattern of inquiry" for an epistemologically conceived reason.

The defining characteristic of all inquiry for Dewey is the problematic situation, which is caused by conflict. The deliberate seeking of knowledge (be it a way to attain food or the resolution to a moral question) implies doubt, uncertainty, and indeterminateness. Inquiry itself arises from a situation of doubt. Dewey defines inquiry as the directed and controlled transformation of a problematic situation to a resolved situation.[17] Resolution as such cannot be spoken of in any determinate way; it is merely the result of the human practice of "considering consequences." Dewey sees the entire scientific enterprise as "an extension and refinement of these simple operations."[18] But these operations are more than mere habit: Dewey is actually positing a view of reason as a type of organic function of being. He states:

> The problematic nature of situations is definitely stated to have its source and prototype in the conditions of imbalance or disequilibrium that recurs rhythmically in the interactivity of organism and environment—a condition exemplified in hunger . . . as a form of organic behavior such as is manifested.[19]

For Dewey, reason as inquiry arises from the problematic situation, and the result of observing and considering consequences is knowledge as the resolved situation. But, as Raymond Boisvert has noted, the scheme rests on an ontological claim in which being is processional, indeterminate, and conflict-ridden.[20] The normative content of the choices available and agreed upon by actual participants cannot be distinguished a priori. The indeterminacy of the resolution does nothing, in practical terms, to rescue publicness from the hands of machines. While admirable, Dewey's pragmatist inclination to avoid making normative claims not devisable from immediately observable practices ultimately rests on identifying reason with an organic and indeterminate process. As a result, inquiry rests on a presocial or prepolitical concept in which the societal and political foundations for his own democratic commitments are passed over.

John Dewey was perhaps the most passionate defender of representative democracy and its reform in his era. His identification of the need for a reinvigorated public as a check on the bureaucratic nation–state and the destabilizing accumulation process is perhaps one of his greatest contributions. Likewise, his desire to avoid epistemological closure only testifies to his commitment to the public's critical function. But, in attempting to ground the public capacity for reason in the flux of inquiry, he offers, ironically, an overly abstract practice that cannot be assumed given the forces he suggests are undermining democracy.

By sketching Dewey's theory of inquiry, it becomes apparent that any theoretical concern for a lack of democratic practice requires an explanation of some scope—one that can address the deformation of the democratic institutions in question and, most importantly, point to a basis for practice that can overcome those problems. Historically, political theorists have most often asserted a notion of reason intended to serve as a defense of the institutionalization of liberal and democratic norms. Their descriptions of reason retain an affinity with the degree and texture of freedom that proposed institutions are presumed to uphold. Traditional understanding of reason has usually provided for a defense of equality by positing universal capacities. But as the conditions of modernity and Dewey rightly suggest, the task of relating such capacities to real political situations can no longer be done "simply in the mind."

The norms modern political theorists have expressed in the simultaneous attachment to reason and democracy have proven to be notoriously undermined by the economic processes, complexity, and instrumental rationality that steer everyday life.[21] In this sense, the curtain has been drawn, exposing both the falsity of liberal grounding schemes *and* modernity's perverse features. Many have considered the revelation sufficient grounds for rejecting the category of reason altogether. This, I argue below, is not only a theoretical mistake, but a practical disaster—especially for progressive social movements. However, the reality brings to light some choices for contemporaries.

On a practical level, in the gap between democratic norms and the self-interested calculations that steer politics, the choices before citizens take three forms: withdrawal, strategic competition, or some alternatively conceived intervention. On a theoretical level, there are three analogous responses to this disjuncture: postmodernism's break with or retreat from Enlightenment ideals altogether; the use of various forms of decision-theoretic, rational-choice approaches; or a reconstruction of those ideals from some alternatively conceived position.

While the overall aim of this book is to help unite the theoretical and practical aspects of an alternatively conceived modernity (vis-à-vis social movements), the remainder of this chapter seeks to explore the potential for reconstructing political criteria in keeping with the most expansive expressions of freedom found in the Enlightenment tradition. Toward this end, and more specifically with regard to the potential role of democratic social movements, I now turn to a discussion of Jurgen Habermas's contribution. It is my contention that both his theory of communicative action and his understanding of the public sphere are important contributions to an emancipatory reconstruction of politics for our era. While his ideas require further practical (institutional and ideological) elaboration so that they may be applied to and by contemporary social movements, his work highlights the stakes in retaining a notion of reason for emancipatory politics.

THE BREAKDOWN OF REASON: MODERNIZATION'S MARIONETTE

There has been no more complete treatment of the notion of reason under modernization than that found in the wide-ranging work of German social theorist Jurgen Habermas. Habermas has attempted nothing less than a metatheoretic, methodological, and empirical critique of reason under the processes of modernization that, according to Thomas McCarthy, "suggests a redirection of rather than an abandonment of the project of the enlightenment."[22] Habermas begins by taking up the Weberian rationalization thesis and by building on the critique of rationalization as reification forwarded by various members of the Frankfurt School. Over the course of more than thirty years, he has sought to recover a notion of reason as "communicative action," which, while providing for the possibility of deploying democratic norms, does so without recourse to the philosophy of history underpinning much of the Frankfurt School's early work. He accomplishes this by locating the potential for communicative reason, not—as Enlightenment thinkers variously do—in transcendental, epistemological, or ontological categories, but "in the structures of action and structures of mutual understanding that are found in the intuitive knowledge of competent members of modern societies."[23]

Habermas's democratic bet rests on the potential for recovery of what politics previously supplied by recourse to philosophical foundations. Methodologically, he is aiming at a pragmatic materialism that frees "historical materialism from its philosophical ballast" by "abstracting the development of cognitive structures from the historical dynamics of events" and "the evolution of society from the historical concretion of forms of life."[24] These real abstractions arise in the course of explanation and serve as the basis for a practical, normative critique without recourse to metaphysical principles.

Habermas identifies four discursive modes through which rational validity claims are asserted within commensurate domains of action—communicative, strategic, normative, and dramaturgic. But among these discursive modes, it is *communicative action* that, in Stephen Bronner's phrase, receives conceptual primacy.[25] Among modernity's discursive modes of argumentation, it is communicative action that Habermas will identify as reflexive and democratically oriented. As a socialized, yet intuitively available mode of argumentation, it simultaneously identifies reason as a normative process with a critical function, while situating it in everyday practices. Set apart from the traditional epistemological problematic of subjective mastery of objective phenomena, communicative rationality focuses on "the intersubjective relation that speaking subjects and acting subjects take up when they come to an understanding with one another about something."[26] Habermas's use of the phrase "coming to an understanding" implies an uncoerced and therefore valid agreement. Such a condition arises from Habermas's abstracted notion of an "ideal speech situation" in which all potential participants must be guaranteed equal access to decisions that affect them. Communicative action, derived from the ideal speech situation, supplies a normative criteria by identifying the "formal properties of action oriented to reaching understanding."[27] As a threatened, yet available, mode of discourse, communicative action provides a way out of the "iron cage." The importance of his contribution toward the recovery of reason comes into focus when considering the critical theory tradition upon which he builds.

Against the increasing pessimism of the Frankfurt School, Habermas sought to identify the effects of modernization processes on "the communicative practice of the everyday lifeworld in which rationality structures are embodied."[28] In *The Theory of Communicative Action, Volume 2*, he sketches his project in comparison to the descriptions and philosophical grounding of Frankfurt School figures such as Adorno, Horkheimer, and Marcuse. Their work, he argues, "placed the consciousness of individuals directly vis-à-vis economic and administrative mechanisms of integration."[29] Moreover, critical theory was still grounded in a Marxist philosophy of history in which the internal dynamics of the production process were considered to be unleashing an "objectively explosive power." But, in the wake of National Socialism and Stalinism, and in the midst of the development of the Keynesian Welfare State, the work of Marcuse, Adorno, and Horkheimer increasingly emphasized the merging of state-administrative and capitalist-accumulation processes in which "a monolithic picture of a totally administered society emerged; corresponding to it was a repressive mode of socialization that shut out inner nature and an omnipresent social control exercised through the channels of mass communication."[30]

Each of the theorists asserted that modernization had resulted in a decreased capacity for subjective, critical comprehension of objective social, political, economic, and cultural processes. This decreased capacity for reflexivity was seen as the hallmark of the era and the death knell of democratic life (and socialist reform) to which they were committed. Aside from Marcuse's later formulation in *One Dimensional Man,* in which he suggests that a slight potential for transformation rests in the consciousness of those at the very margins of society,[31] essentially the Frankfurt School's leading figures were more and more convinced that, according to Habermas, "in the totally administered society only instrumental rationality, expanded into a totality, found embodiment."[32]

Such pessimism ensued despite critical theory's early intentions. In his inaugural lecture at the Institute for Social Research in 1930, Max Horkhiemer posed the project this way:

In a definite time frame and in some particular countries, what relations can we delineate between a particular social group and the role of this group in the economy, the changes in the psychic structure of its members, and the thoughts and institutions created by it which influence it as a whole through the social totality?[33]

The critique of instrumental reason forwarded by Frankfurt School figures—tied as it was to a philosophy of history in which culture, consciousness, and reason as such were increasingly reified—provided only negative answers to the research proposal mentioned above. Habermas's tack has been to identify contradictory tendencies in which modernization processes (i.e., the capitalist accumulation process and state-administrative rationalization) while "anchored" in the lifeworld, can be differentiated not only from each other but from those elements of the lifeworld that clash with system demands.

The concept of the lifeworld as such "refers to the totality of sociocultural facts" or the "cognitive reference system" against which narrating subjects make claims and reach mutual understanding. For Habermas, the lifeworld is not a simple manifestation of repressive forces, but is also the bearer of independent communication structures that exist beyond the demands of system integration. While the threat of a "colonized" lifeworld remains, processes in which mutual understanding must occur remain as part of the lifeworld. As a result of systemic tendencies toward the privatization and secularization of sociocultural modes, the lifeworld becomes uncoupled from system integration and presents opportunities for communicative action.

By positing an uncoupling of system and action spheres, Habermas simultaneously recovers a normative and practical opening for reform. In considering the potential for protest in "welfare-state mass democracies," Habermas contends that new conflicts appear to arise "along the seams between system and lifeworld." This is where the demands of the economic and administrative action systems (via the media of money and power) extend ever more pressure (or toxicity in the case of environmental pressures) for competition and performance on the institutionalized roles of private persons. But, as Habermas notes, the evidence of resistance is not tantamount to the hope for progressive reform.

Progressive resistance is evident when, as Kenneth Tucker has observed, the "uninstitutionalized counterfactual potential" of communicative rationality emerges from within the lifeworld. Social movements based on "non-coercive participatory and universalistic precepts" are thus examples of lifeworld expression of communicative action.[34] Yet, just as the lifeworld is threatened by instrumental and strategic rationality, so too is the potential for such movements. The tentative potential of communicative action (and social movements) is captured in Habermas's work of the public sphere.

It is my contention that the analytic usefulness of the concept of communicative action requires connecting it up to empirical movements in historically specified situations. As such, it supplies useful criteria for distinguishing among types of movements and can aid in interpreting so-called defeats and victories. Ultimately, however, its practical emergence rests on the development of a reflexive movement ideology that grasps the relationship between communicative action and the institutionalized (economic and political) preconditions for its exercise. In this sense, Habermas's notion of the endangered public sphere offers important, albeit abstract, cues for contemporary movements.

SOCIAL MOVEMENTS AS PUBLIC SPHERE: HABERMAS'S CONTRIBUTION

Habermas's 1962 work, *The Structural Transformation of the Public Sphere* (only translated into English in 1989), is a critical evaluation of "a category of bourgeois society." As such, the public sphere is seen as an historical phenomenon that "grew out of a specific phase of bourgeois society and could enter into the order of the bourgeois constitutional state only as a result of a particular constellation of interests."[35]

It was not until the emergence of early finance capital and trade capitalism beginning in the thirteenth century, and the eventual appearance of market networks, trade fairs, and stock exchanges in the sixteenth century, that horizontal economic relationships emerged that challenged the "vertical relationships of dependence characterizing the organization of domination in the estate system and household economy."[36] This emerging fissure, widening into the seventeenth century, eventually became the space between private life and the state or what is termed civil society. Alongside the traffic in commodities, the "traffic in news" sprung up, and in time, the press developed into a powerful influence for the emerging liberal regimes. The public sphere that emerged, Habermas contends, can be conceived "as the sphere of private people come together as a public" in which deliberation on public matters "mediates between society and the state."[37] Its potential could be found in its critical function represented by its aim toward debate where "people's public use of their reason" has made possible "the democratic control of the state."[38]

Empirically speaking, however, the bourgeois public sphere was controlled by bourgeois men in their effort to engage public authorities in

debate over the "general rules governing relations in the basically privatized but publicly relevant sphere of commodity exchange and social
labor."[39] Their political and economic successes cast a paradoxical net
over the public sphere; the liberal constitutional guarantees for free speech
and association that underpin the public sphere are threatened by the instrumental and strategic interests of the same industrializing class that
brought it into being. As Habermas's critics have emphasized, other "basically privatized but publicly relevant" arenas of life were excluded from
the historical public sphere.

We also know that multiple "publics" existed: literary or salon publics,
as Joan Landes's work points out, emerged and waned;[40] "plebeian
publics," such as those evident in the anarchist and Chartist Movements,
flourished and were crushed; slave publics, where revolts were discussed
and underground routes organized; and successive female publics, such as
women-led revolts in the streets of eighteenth-century Paris demanding
bread. While public opinion grew, legal, economic, and custom-based exclusions expanded as well. As property became a legally enforced precondition for citizenship, the critical function of public opinion diminished. But for Habermas, these acknowledged exclusions do not diminish
the potential to be found in the legacy of the public sphere.

Habermas's work documents the structural transformation of the critical potential of the public sphere into a kind of false publicity under the
modernizing forces of instrumental rationalization and commodification.
At the same time, Habermas remains committed to tracing the pathways
of a repressed use of public reason. He locates public sphere potential in
the lifeworld—away from the state and the economy. Where conditions
are met that approximate the critical conditions of the ideal public
sphere,[41] so too we discover the use of communicative action.

It follows that social movements, as expressions of lifeworld conflicts,
are a potential arena or public sphere for the development and expression
of communicative action. To the extent that they embrace the rules for
public debate (general accessibility, elimination of all privilege, and the
discovery of general norms and rational legitimations), they offer resistance to the threat of the "colonization of the lifeworld."

The problems presented by this formulation are numerous. Even if we
grant the possibility of communicative action emerging as an ideological
frame for social movements, social movements themselves are precari-
ously caught between a threatened lifeworld and the systemic imperatives
of (1) the accumulation process and (2) the paradoxical administrative

state on whose constitutional guarantees, welfare function, and legislative potential their success depends. Social movements, as expressions of the lifeworld, cannot therefore conceive of themselves as something apart from, or fundamentally opposed to, the traditional state. In addition, that the lifeworld issues brought forth by social movements and the obstacles to successful organizing stem from tendencies in the accumulation process must also be confronted. The only practical arena for a confrontation of both administrative- and accumulation-based "distortions" is, I contend, the state itself.

Social movements' ability to sustain themselves and serve a critical function is contingent on halting the further encroachment of economic and bureaucratic pressures. We know from the sixties experience that the symbolic presentation of issues alone is an insufficient guard against such encroachment (see chapter 4, "Interest-Group Liberalism and the Rise of Cultural Politics"). Developing a mode of interaction that preserves movements' critical function, while navigating (transforming?) the political terrain upon which their success depends requires operating both strategically and communicatively. As I try to show later in this book, the organizational and ideological demands of such a task are profoundly difficult to navigate in reality.

If progressive social movements are to offer any hope for significantly easing the manifold burdens on ordinary people, their precarious position must be realistically considered. What modernity assures us is that the contingency of democratic norms and capacities as expressed in Habermas's communicative action *requires institutional backing* for their preservation and further development. While Habermas's notion of social movements as potential public spheres provides a normative and procedural model, its embodiment among social movements requires three things: a reflexive awareness on the part of social movements of their own precarious position vis-à-vis the systemic context; the translation of that awareness into a workable movement ideology; and the ability to retain both strategic and communicative modes organizationally and reflexively. The ability of social movements to operationalize these insights is additionally complicated by more or less favorable national traditions with respect to both political culture and state and institutional patterns.

It is important to acknowledge that not all institutional context in "welfare mass democracies" are the same; as such, Habermas's generalizations about the administrative state requires further specification. In the next chapter I argue that the particular constraints of the historical American state have presented more obstacles to progressive social movement success (defined both normatively and strategically) than in comparable nations. Ideological traditions, revealed in the interplay between movements and the state, place progressive social movements at a particular disadvantage when it comes to articulating systemic constraints. In addition, due to limited institutional points of access and accountability (increasingly so in the post–New Deal context), social movements in America have frequently been unable to secure guarantees for their further expansion. Lockian-inspired individualism, the Federalist design, and the two-party system are among the reasons. Historically speaking, where democratic and egalitarian demands have been advanced and call into question the negative aspects of industrialization, movements found themselves institutionally frustrated, attacked, or co-opted. Social reform movements in the bourgeois era paradoxically instigated additional political controls on social movement influence.

In the next chapter I take a look at the ways in which American ideology, the framers' design, and historical social movement challenges have shaped subsequent social movement repertoires.

NOTES

1. Most exemplary of this position is perhaps Francois Lyotard (*The Postmodern Condition*), but the same skepticism is evident in the works of Michel Foucault, Jaques Derrida, and Richard Rorty.

2. Here I am referring to those theses that suggest a convergence of economic and state modes under an encompassing administrative rationality that attacks reflexivity. Roughly similar versions of this thesis can be seen in the works of such diverse authors as T. W. Adorno, Herbert Marcuse, Ernesto Laclau and Chantal Mouffe, Alberto Melucci, and Alain Touraine.

3. See Frances Fukuyama, "The End of History?" in *The National Interest*, Summer 1989.

4. Among the many journalistic and academic works published since 1995 are Sarah Diamond, *Roads to Dominion: Right Wing Movements and Political Power in the United States* (New York: Guilford Press, 1995); Herbert Kitchelt, *The Radical Right in Western Europe* (Ann Arbor: University of Michigan Press, 1995); Valerie Jenness and Kendal Broad, *Hate Crimes: New Social Movements and the Politics of Violence* (New York: Aldine Greyter, 1997); Aurel Braun and Stephen Scheinberg, *The Extreme Right: Freedom and Security at Risk* (New York: Westview Press, 1997); Kenneth Stern, *A Force upon the Plain: The American Militia Movement and the Politics of Hate* (New York: Simon & Schuster, 1996); and a host of American militia movement titles.

5. See *The Structural Transformation of the Public Sphere* (Cambridge: MIT Press, 1982) and *Between Facts and Norms* (Cambridge: MIT Press, 1996).

6. See Ben Barber's *Jihad Versus McWorld* (New York: Ballantine, 1996).

7. In the Habermasian sense, I am referring to an intermediary deliberative sphere between state and private life that is substantively accessible to all participants affected by the policies debated.

8. Jurgen Habermas, *The Theory of Communicative Action, Volume One: Reason and Rationalization of Society* (Boston: Beacon Press, 1984), p. 4.

9. See Max Horkheimer's critique of the idea of a universal scientific method applicable to both the natural and the social sciences in "The Latest Attack on Metaphysics" and "Traditional and Critical Theory" in *Critical Theory: Selected Essays* (New York: Herder & Herder, 1972).

10. MacPherson, *Possessive Individualism* (Oxford: Oxford University Press, 1962), p. 12.

11. Ibid., p. 30.

12. Hobbes, *Leviathan* (New York: Viking Penguin, 1985), p. 85.

13. Ibid., p. 111.

14. Patrick Neal, "In the Shadow of the General Will: Rawls, Kant, and Rousseau on the Problem of Political Right," in *The Review of Politics* (1988), p. 392.

15. Immanuel Kant, *Groundwork of the Metaphysics of Morals* (New York: Harper Torchbooks, 1959), p. 70.

16. John Dewey, *Characters and Events: Popular Essays in Social and Political Philosophy,* ed. Joseph Ratner, (New York: Henry Holt, 1929), pp. 255–256.

17. George Dicker, *Dewey's Theory of Knowing* (Philadelphia: Philosophical Monographs, 1976), p. 9.

18. John Dewey, *The Quest for Certainty* (New York: Capricorn Books, 1960), p. 123.

19. John Dewey, *The Problems of Men* (New York: Greenwood Press, 1968), p. 350, Cf. *Logic: The Theory of Inquiry* (New York: Rheinhart and Winston, 1938), p. 26–27.

20. See Raymond Boisvert, *Dewey's Metaphysics* (New York: Fordham University Press, 1988).

21. Jurgen Habermas, *The Theory of Communicative Rationality,* vol. 2 (Boston: Beacon Press, 1984).

22. "Translator's Introduction" from *The Theory of Communicative Action,* vol. 1 (Boston: Beacon Press, 1984), p. viii.

23. Jurgen Habermas, "The Tasks of a Critical Social Theory," in *Jurgen Habermas on Society and Politics* (Boston: Beacon Press, 1989), p. 84.

24. Jurgen Habermas, "The Tasks of a Critical Theory of Society," in Jurgen *Habermas on Society and Politics* (Boston: Beacon Press, 1989), p. 84.

25. Stephen Bronner, *Of Critical Theory and Its Theorists* (Cambridge: Blackwell, 1994), p. 295.

26. Habermas, *Theory of Communicative Rationality,* vol. 1 (Boston: Beacon Press, 1984), p. 392.

27. Ibid., p. 392.

28. *Habermas on Society and Politics* (Boston: Beacon Press, 1989), p. 84.

29. Ibid., p. 84.

30. Ibid., p. 82.

31. In *One Dimensional Man* (Boston: Beacon Press, 1964), he locates this potential consciousness among "the outcasts and outsiders, the exploited and persecuted of other races and other colours, the unemployed and the unemployable."

32. Habermas, "The Tasks of a Critical Theory of Society," p. 83.

33. Max Horkheimer, "The State of Contemporary Social Philosophy and the Tasks of an Institute for Social Research" (trans. Peter Wagner) in *Critical Theory and Society*, Stephen Bronner and Douglas Kellner, eds. (New York: Routledge, 1989), p. 34.

34. Kenneth Tucker, "Ideology and Social Movements: The Contributions of Habermas" in *Sociological Inquiry*, vol. 59, n.1 (1989), pp. 38–39.

35. Jurgen Habermas "The Public Sphere: An Encyclopedia Article" in *New German Critique*, vol. 1, n. 3 (1974), p. 50.

36. Habermas, *The Structural Transformation of the Public Sphere* (Cambridge: MIT Press, 1989), p. 15.

37. Ibid., p. 50.

38. Ibid., p. 50.

39. Ibid., p. 27.

40. I disagree, however, with Landes's entire line of argument in which the empirical fact of women-led salons is taken as an emancipatory inheritance for women. In *Women and the Public Sphere in the Age of the French Revolution*, her claim that the bourgeois public sphere was more "pervasively" gendered than that of the court exaggerates the degree (and source of) power the semi-aristocratic, semi-bourgeois ladies of the salon wielded. It also ignores the constitutional (bourgeois) basis of women's eventual liberation struggles.

41. Editor Peter Hohendahl, in a footnote to the original encyclopedia article, stipulated these conditions as (1) general accessibility, (2) elimination of all privileges, and (3) the discovery of general norms and rational legitimations.

PART TWO

Social Movements
and the American Context

Chapter Three

Locke, Stock, and Barricades

A philosopher, it is true, might look askance at the theory of power the Americans developed. It was not a model of lucid exposition. The trouble lay with their treatment of sovereignty. Instead of boldly rejecting the concept, as Franklin was once on the verge of doing when he said it made him "quite sick," they accepted the concept and tried to qualify it out of existence.

Louis Hartz[1]

New social movements are in no small measure pragmatically tied to the institutional and ideological histories of the context in which they emerge. At the same time, as I argued in earlier chapters, national ideologies and institutional patterns are conditioned by large-scale systemic processes. If "new" social movements can be said to be both *a result and a rejection of* the broader, instrumental forces associated with modernity, their potential for bringing those aspects of modernity under democratic control is significantly tied to an awareness of the institutional and ideological features of their national political traditions as well. Without an understanding of how institutions and ideological traditions condition social movement forms, movements themselves will be unable to reflexively adopt appropriate norms and procedures for navigating the dual pressures of integration v. marginalization. New social movements in America are particularly vulnerable in this regard; the accumulation process and administrative prerogatives have historically remained outside the purview of democratic control. In other words, the two main threats to democracy in our era have been particularly advantaged in America. A reflection on the history of the American ideological and institutional context in relation to popular challenges can illustrate this disadvantage.

If, as Louis Hartz suggests, a "philosopher might look askance at the theory of power the Americans developed," the history of social movements in America only illustrates why. Theories of power, to be sure, are meaningful only to the extent that they are expressed in institutions, ideology, and practice. The early American outlook—premised on Lockian liberalism and a Federalist design bent on the diffusion of popular control—has cast a long and debilitating shadow on social movements seeking to expand economic and political accountability. That long shadow was reshaped in the nineteenth and twentieth centuries by the shoring up of electoral restraints and the rise of the administrative state with its attendant notions of pluralist representation. It is a penumbra that continues to shadow new social movements that find themselves tangled up in the ideological and political implications of interest-group liberalism.[2]

The situation of NSMs today, perhaps surprisingly, may be elucidated by a fresh appraisal of Hartz's thesis. Indeed, I argue that the ideological and institutional predecessors of interest-group liberalism are Lockian liberalism and Hamiltonian and Madisonian institutional designs. In combination, these founding forces sought to restrain the "factional" politics of popular control. This is not to say that varieties of social movements—Right, Left, and Center—have not escaped the boundaries intended. Indeed, in many respects, the history of the U.S. state is a history significantly shaped by popular challenges—be they religious, racial, agrarian, feminist, moralist, or economic in character. Yet, the most pressing meaning of these challenges, at least in relation to the potential of democratic social movements today, is not to be found in their particular legislative victories, organizational histories, and even bloody defeats.

Many U.S. movements have been successful without seriously altering the stubborn ideological and institutional tendencies that support elite interests. While this may seem a narrow criterion that undervalues the rich historical contributions of some of America's most passionate (or notorious) movements, it does not seek to deny the breadth and diversity of U.S. social movements historically. Instead, by focusing on what happens when movements mount ideological and institutional challenges to the most persistent obstacles to critical public control, important legacies are revealed. These legacies are discovered in the interplay between social movements and the state. Out of this interplay, from both perspectives, repertoires of understanding are forged and passed along. Of course, from the perspective of the state, those understandings have far greater force. This has led me to focus on challenges that have addressed both economic disadvantage and political representation. Such a focus tells a story of often-heroic movements, when not simply being attacked, suffering the effects of diffusion, integration, or destruction amid the complex institutional patterns of "legitimate" politics. The movements for political and economic justice of the nineteenth and early twentieth centuries in the United States—among them socialism, Populism, and Progressivism—attempted to stretch the ideological and institutional imagination of America but ultimately revealed the adaptability of the system. While all three movements demonstrated a faith in the democratic promise of America, each movement was denuded of elements that questioned the inegalitarian and undemocratic tendencies expressed in economic policies, institutions, and founding ideologies. Specifically, where political and economic privilege were challenged, the movements were met with either repression or integration. Each of these movements, to different degrees, challenged Lockian liberalism and Federalist limits on representation. And each had significant elements of those challenges rejected as extreme.

What has been labeled extreme in America, however, is usually standard fare among the legitimate parties of Western Europe and other capitalist democracies that evidence either a broader ideological tradition or a multi-party, proportional system of representation. Yet, in the United States, where Lockian liberalism glorifies individual rights in market terms—fully equating democracy with capitalism—and the institutional arrangements limit the impact of organized individuals upon governmental processes as a matter of principle, it is no surprise that movements as diverse as socialism, Populism, and Progressivism should not fit through the eye of the American needle. The emergence of the two-party system, with its buttressing electoral arrangements, secured these limits and established new boundaries on the imagination of social movements.

These three social movements in the United States navigated a terrain defined by a narrow ideological tradition and a restrictive institutional context. Most importantly, the history of the interaction between these movements and American institutions has produced a limited and contradictory repertoire of social movement ideologies and practices. The history of these three challenges support a legacy in which radical impulses bear the stamp of marginality. At the same time, social movement legacies retain a critical, radical potential as well. Unfortunately, social movements in the nineteenth and twentieth centuries often internalized their marginality and, to the degree that they remain unable to secure institutional influence, have drifted further away from thematizing claims in relation to state centers of power. In this sense, what is "new" in social movements today has substantial roots in historical exclusions.

BETWEEN LOCKE AND A HARD PLACE: LIBERAL IDEOLOGY AND THE FRAMERS' DESIGN

The narrowness of the American ideological tradition is in large part a result of the historical commitment to the Lockian world view. That narrowness is also by now a matter of fixed reality, institutionalized in the electoral arrangements and buttressed by the pluralism of interest-group politics. Historically, where a serious threat to the stability of these arrangements arose, adjustments were made, and at times, limited and often temporary gains won. But each partial redress has had its defensive component as well. Just as vaccination yields viral immunity, a small threat is often absorbed by the institutional body in an effort to stave off larger and more profound incursions. And within the American tradition, social movements that sought to expand political access for workers and the poor in an effort to establish social democracy and economic justice were perceived as just such a threat. The American version of Lockian liberalism, in the context of Madisonian politics and Hamiltonian institutional designs, sets the stage for nineteenth- and early-twentieth-century social movement diffusion. This diffusion has significantly shaped the repertoires available to later social movements.

The narrow ideological tradition in American is made clear by the lack of a strong socialist or social democratic tradition. By comparison, European countries have been home to popular socialist movements and a wide range of social democratic parties and policies that have fundamentally influenced state power. The relationships between European institutional structures, liberalism, and socialism are far reaching when compared with the American scenario. Theories seeking to explain this difference are varied, but, as Louis Hartz legitimately claims, the absence of a strong socialist or social democratic tradition in America has simultaneously meant that "there has never been a 'liberal movement' or a real 'liberal' party in America"[3] either. Not only is America missing a socialist tradition, it is missing a truly liberal tradition as well. Hartz's claim centers on the lack of emphasis on popular controls in American ideology and institutions as compared with European politics. It is my claim that this absence, its causes, and its manifestations has profoundly constrained the impact of social movements in America and conditioned many of those characteristics NSM theorists attributed to global shifts.

Various theories have been advanced to explain America's divergence from Europe and to account for the "exceptional" political landscape in the United States. The failure of left-wing movements to sink roots in the United States has concerned sympathetic intellectuals and social movement participants alike. Beginning with Werner Sombart in 1906, socialism's absence in America was premised on the notion that America's working class was too well off to breed proletarian revolution. Sombart also pointed to a combination of other factors unique to the American situation, including open frontiers, political structures that served as barriers, possibilities for class mobility, and the relatively high standard of living enjoyed by American workers.[4]

Variations on Sombart's thesis have been picked up and reformulated. Some of these important contributions have highlighted the unique vulnerability of the American working class to divisions along racial and ethnic lines.[5] Other theorists have raised single-factor explanations, which tend to isolate economic, political, and ideological influences.[6] Ironically, Louis Hartz, in his influential work, *The Liberal Tradition in America* (1955), admits to engaging in a single-factor analysis by asserting that the absence of feudalism defines the American liberal experience. This is ironic, I suggest, because in Hartz's thesis there is enormous explanatory power that permits a type of coherence between economic, political, and ideological factors seldom seen in competing theories. As John Diggins commented, "One of the great achievements of Hartz's *The Liberal Tradition in America* is that it succeeded in doing what Marxists have long encouraged scholars to do even though they themselves seldom do it: combine an analysis of the social structure with an analysis of the political ideology that emanates from it."[7]

Louis Hartz suggests that a lack of feudalism, combined with an "irrational" attachment to Lockian individualism, produced an intolerance for socialism—and social conflict in general. Hartz argues that because of the absence of feudalism in the colonies, the American Revolution did not necessitate a national democratic revolution against an ancien régime. In addition, because religious forces were not only allied with the American Revolution, but were a galvanizing force, there was no need to create a civil "religion" as in the movements of Europe. As Hartz put it, "Thus, the American liberals, instead of being forced to pull the Christian heaven down to earth, were glad to leave it where it was. They did not need to make a religion out of the revolution because religion was already revolutionary."[8] Able to escape the need to centralize authority against a centralized feudal regime, uninterested in the civil religion of the Enlightenment, already "born equal" as Tocqueville would have it, the American revolutionaries wedded themselves to a kind of Lockian liberalism built on natural rights, the rewards of hard work, and a distrust of state authority.

Without the onslaught of the ancien régime, Hartz argues, no socialism appears. Socialism, Hartz argues, is a "largely ideological phenomena," and it appears not simply to fight capitalism but the vestiges of feudalism as well. Thus, the appearance of so-called natural liberalism senses no need for the concept of class: "For if the concept of class was meaningless in its Disraelian form, and if American liberalism had never acquired it in its bourgeois form, why should it be any more meaningful in its Marxian form?"[9] In contrast to European "liberals," the American liberal had no aristocrats to struggle against; as a result, they had no opportunity to ally with the working class and vice versa. Liberalism in America, it would follow, lacks insight into its own class character, for it never becomes an issue. The impression of social and economic unanimity, *and* the belief in divine individuality, become inscribed on the American liberal mind.

Locke in America is not without his paradoxes. If Locke is the backdrop for Jeffersonian democracy, he serves as the veil for Hamiltonian and Madisonian controls on democracy. On the one hand, we understand Locke's influence on America in the Jeffersonian claims that "man was a rational animal endowed by nature with rights and with an innate sense of justice" who could be "restrained from wrong and protected in rights by moderate powers confided to persons of his own choice." And, as Jefferson scholar Joseph Ellis noted, though indebted to Locke, Jefferson's political vision was more radical than liberal, driven as it was by a youthful romanticism unwilling to negotiate its high standards with an imperfect world.[10]

Indeed, Ellis also observes that the sentimental reading Jefferson gives Locke is captured in his choosing the "felicitous" phrase *pursuit of happiness*[11] and dropping *property*. Whereas Jefferson blurs the contradictions implied by a humanistic natural rights premised on property rights (including slavery), Hamilton and Madison more straightforwardly render

Locke's "other" meaning in institutional terms. In recasting Hartz, we can say that whereas Jefferson's Locke is taken up rhetorically and ideologically, the Federalists' Locke becomes embodied in the state.

Clearly, Locke's shadow casts a different silhouette on Alexander Hamilton who, when proposing life terms for senators, suggested "all communities divide themselves into the few and the many. The first are rich and well-born and the other the mass of people who seldom judge or determine right."[12] The Antifederalist charge of aristocrat against the Federalists does not seem so farfetched when confronted with the Federalists' concern that the Confederation produced the instability of mass rule. Hartz sees the problem between the Federalists and Antifederalists as a conflict between those who embraced Lockianism in a land without its main enemy, and those who, like Hamilton, were actually "frustrated liberals who want to lean on a bit of aristocracy."[13] More specifically, the Federalists really were aiming for the elements of central control necessitated by the demands of an emerging national capitalist economy. While it may be useful to see them as semi-aristocratic and semi-bourgeois, it is more important to see how they inspired, to borrow Hartz's phrase, a new "frustrated liberalism."

This frustrated liberalism is evident in the well-documented Madisonian anxiety about factions. Perhaps Madison provides a clearer understanding of the Federalist desire for limiting popular control. From the start, Madison sees factions as necessarily contrary to the aims of government as he and the Federalists define them. Using words like "dangerous vice" and "mortal disease," Madison elaborates in *Federalist* No. 10 his views regarding the nature, cause, and cure of this threat to stable government:

> By faction, I understand a number of citizens, whether amounting to a majority or minority of the whole, who are united and actuated by some common impulse of passion, or of interest, adverse to the rights of other citizens, or to the permanent and aggregate interests of the community.[14]

Having established that a faction is defined in opposition to the rights of others and to the general interests of the community, Madison suggests the real source of threat he seeks to protect "government" from:

> The most common and durable source of faction has been the various and unequal distribution of property. Those who hold and those who are without property have ever formed distinct interests in society. The regulation of these various interests forms the principal task of modern legislation and

involves the spirit of party and faction in the necessary and ordinary operations of government.[15]

Relief from faction is to be accomplished, in the Federalist view, by means of a republican form of government that limits the impact of majority faction based on class (in Madison's eyes, clearly the rebellious debtors of Shays' persuasion) through the mechanisms of federalism, bicameralism, and indirect election for most major offices. Among the features of the new regime, only the franchise would appear truly democratic. Yet its limits were fixed in the constitutional arrangements described above, and in electoral "engineering" that had the effect of narrowing electoral participation, even as the formal franchise was being widened.[16] As preconceived limits on the democratic mass, institutional and electoral arrangements situated the organized movements for extended political and economic rights of the nineteenth and early twentieth centuries upon a terrain that was at best unfriendly, and at worst (and frequently it was) violent in its opposition.

At the same time, in the Federalist v. Antifederalist debates, the choice was never really between the ruling class and the laboring class, as Charles Beard seems to suggest. Jefferson's more purely Lockian vision of the automatic state, small in scale and dependent on popular consent, was earnestly embodied in the comparatively radical availability of the franchise and in the composition of the newly created state legislatures under the Articles of Confederation. But, for the reasons Hartz argues, these farmers and merchants in preindustrial America represented a proto-middle class unlike the bourgeoisie in Europe. Nonetheless, there were popular sentiments among this class that the Federalists desired to contain. The Federalists (and later the Whigs) represented, in Hartz's view, "all the nonliberal European elements that the American world has liberalized and inspirited with the ethos of Sydney and Locke."[17] Foremost among the Federalist intentions was the establishment of a national capitalist economy (a version of the economy that inspired Locke) to be accomplished through what Hamilton, in a speech to the New York ratifying convention, called "strength and stability in the organization of our government, and vigor in its operations."[18] This stability, and the interests it sought to protect, comprise the heart of the Federalist designs for limited popular sovereignty.

The period between the Articles of Confederation and the ratification of the second Constitution was filled with strife and bubbling social and economic discontent. As John Diggins noted, the volatile post-Revolutionary era, in which class tensions arose, induced fear in the Federalists like Madison and John Adams, who abandoned the Lockian man for a Hobbesian view with class conflict as the biggest threat.[19]

Jefferson, warning against those Federalists who would eventually use the rebellion as a justification for, in Joseph Ellis's phrase "more coercive political institutions," wrote to William Stephens Smith that they were "sending up a kite to keep the hen yard in order."[20] But, as it turned out, they sent up more than a kite.

Shays' Rebellion on the one hand, and, for example, the Federalist denunciations of the French Revolution on the other, suggest two trends in American political life that frame American liberal ideology: the radicalism of rebellious farmers and the fear it induced among the merchant and governing classes. Both impulses belong to American liberalism. They are mediated by the institutions crafted by Hamilton and Madison. At the same time, Jeffersonian Lockianism informs the practical understanding and rhetoric of the nation. Like a veil, it obscures the limits on popular control. For Hartz, this is nothing more than a "hidden and happy accident." He suggests that the "Founding Fathers devised a scheme to deal with conflict that could only survive in a land of solidarity. The truth is, their conclusions were 'right' only because their premises were wrong."[21]

The Hartzian version of Lockian liberalism in America describes a consensus that has never been fully complete. If not, then why were the Federalist fears of mass insurrection so pronounced? Yet Hartz is of course largely correct. The Federalist institutional design, replete with checks and balances, indirectly elected representatives, and dual federalism was effective not because it was designed for a literal "land of solidarity,"[22] but because it protected the interests of an emerging national economy before it protected popular control. That it was wrapped up in the rhetorical promises of Jefferson means only that in actual fact, the nonpropertied masses were left between Locke and a hard place. But it is best to demonstrate the predominance of both trends (Lockian individualism and Federalist-designed institutional limits on popular control) in the context of social movements seeking to expand political rights and economic justice. Below, I consider the interplay between socialism, Populism, and Progressivism and the American state in relation to these constraints. And while my selection of and (my admittedly broad) reflections on these movements may appear to diminish the scope and variety

of movement activity of the nineteenth and early twentieth centuries un-
duly, I am suggesting that these movements, in relation to the constraints
I've thematized, provide considerable insight into the ability of subsequent movements to expand possibilities for democratic control of the
state and, as such, economic life.

I contend that these nineteenth- and twentieth-century social movements seeking to expand the economic and political rights of marginalized
sectors of society illustrate the pervasive impact of Lockian liberalism and
the institutional restraints on popular movement demands. The three
movements discussed below demonstrate that social movements here are
constrained not only by the same structural shifts in transnational capitalism experienced by commensurate European challenges, but also by (in
the first case) a national ideology of Lockian liberalism. Indeed, movements here are both constrained and inspired by this complex ideological
tradition. This, I argue, can be seen in the translation of the radical impulses of each movement into a Lockian faith in the individual's chance
or bargain with capitalism. On this count, the dedication to individual
rights and equal economic opportunity (especially among Populists)
grounds their notions of fairness. This, I suggest later, makes each movement susceptible to integration.

Institutionally, as well, these movements are simultaneously inspired
and constrained. Apart from the relative availability of and early enthusiasm for the franchise, little else institutionally supports the democratic impulses of these movements on the American political landscape. In addition to dual federalism and the Hamiltonian separation of powers aimed at
diffusing popular interests, I argue that social movements also had to contend with the Madisonian anxiety over class-based factions as the contradictory history of party co-optation, contraction of the franchise, and other
electoral "reforms" illustrate. Ultimately, in the interplay between movements and the state, we discover renewed controls on popular social
movements.

Socialism, Populism, and Progressivism, I suggest, all interact with
formal institutions; however, while some shift in the dominant paradigm
may have occurred, they did not (from the state's perspective) secure
movement influence in the future (i.e., electoral reform). Likewise, little
was contributed to the repertoires of social movements' action and ideology that would suggest contestational strategies for substantive and secured institutional reform.

Around and within these arrangements floats an ideological attachment to liberalism without substantive rights—an attachment that is simultaneously, if not paradoxically, challenged by and internalized by the social movements. These founding constraints help focus contemporary reflections on social movements and the American state. By reflecting on this interplay within a frame that highlights the most exclusionary ideological and institutional limits of the state, movements' self-understandings and repertoires of action gain a new significance that can help us untangle the parameters of subsequent challenges.

AMERICAN DIALECTIC: REFLECTIONS ON SOCIAL MOVEMENTS AND THE AMERICAN STATE

At first blush, the American movements for socialism, Populism, and Progressivism seem incompatible. Yet the absence of a socialist politic, that distinguishing feature of American exceptionalism, in many ways makes the other two movements more comprehensible. The early socialist movement in America, the subsequent interactions between Populists and socialists, then Progressives and socialists, and the resultant ideological legacies for social movements to follow, are all conditioned and informed by the parameters of Lockian liberalism and Federalist-inspired restraints on organized interests. The three movements also offer a look at three major episodes in American history that, to varying degrees of success and failure, involved mobilizations for institutional, political, and economic reform.

Each of these movements, from very different bases, has demanded an extension of democratic and economic rights to marginalized sectors of American society. Each movement has engaged in both intra- and extra-institutional practices as a means of gaining leverage. Each reflects a thwarted impulse that in some measure was absorbed and transformed under the persuasive, even coercive, force of American liberalism and the institutional limits on popular control. And each has contributed to the ideological and institutional developments that confronted social movements following the Second World War. The dialogues between them, while interesting, testify to the limited institutional access available to democratic social movements in the United States. These dialogues also form the foundation of the ideological repertoires available to social movements that followed.

SOCIALISM: INSCRUTABLE AMERICA

In the period between the constitutional founding of the United States of America and the Civil War, class antagonisms did percolate. The particular conditions of the American Revolution—its lack of a feudal enemy and its unique liberal stance—made it far more difficult for early industrial workers and artisans to organize themselves against what Mike Davis has called "the special gift of liberty that God and Locke had granted their Puritan ancestors."[23] Still, evidence suggests that class concerns did clearly emerge in nineteenth-century American social movements. Such is the significance of the well-known Workingman's Parties of 1828–1832, which made decent electoral showings in several cities in the East during those years.[24]

Both Marx and Engels celebrated the Workingman's Party as the world's very first organized political party of labor. Marx and Engels also took stock of the unique situation the new nation presented to workers. But, unlike twentieth-century American critics, Marx and Engels initially heralded these "exceptions" and saw great promise in the American working class. Nonetheless, socialism did not prevail or take root in a manner comparable to Europe. So much has been offered as explanation to the question first posed by Werner Sombart in his essay "Why Is There No Socialism in America?" Much of the literature agrees, to varying extent, that the ideological constraints imposed by American Lockian liberalism and the institutional barriers to "factions" were among the factors that prohibited the constitution of an autonomous working-class politic.[25]

The experience of American labor in the first half of the nineteenth century testifies to the ideological and institutional obstacles encountered by social movements struggling for democratic and economic reform. Even the heralded franchise seemed incapable of guaranteeing policy as the working-class gains made in elections were undermined. First, as inroads were made, ideological faith in the franchise was met with state interventions, thus halting the emergence of a socialist politic. Mike Davis contends:

> From the mid-1830s onwards, journeymen in the big port cities began to assert their separate economic interests, organizing their own benefit societies and early trade unions. Over the next two decades the center of gravity of this union movement began to shift either to skilled workers in the new mechanized industries like the cotton spinners and shoemakers, or towards

the craftsmen who made machines. . . . Unfortunately, their efforts were rewarded by few permanent successes: the broad Ten Hour Day agitation of the 1840s rose and fell, a first generation of trade unions perished in the panic of 1837, a second in the Depression of 1857, and, finally, on the eve of the Civil War, the most powerful trade union in North America—the New England Merchant's Association (shoemakers)—was crushed after a long strike.[26]

The emerging era of monopolies conflicted with the egalitarianism stressed by the American labor movement. The Lockian attachment to property, it would seem, overwhelmed the emerging ideological challenge based on economic egalitarianism. Oddly enough, working-class egalitarianism in America, informed as it was by the socialist tradition, was nonetheless affected by the Lockian liberal tradition. The result was a split consciousness on the part of the American socialist movement—periodically unified, militant, and articulate on issues of class on the one hand, yet politically tied to an individualist faith in liberty symbolized by the franchise. As a seemingly legitimate connection, the electoral link between the two positions was undermined in a maze of institutional diffusion under federal and electoral arrangements. The early working-class movement was seduced by the popular view of the state as an agent of democratic reform. Unlike their European counterparts, who at this time were struggling for political rights alongside bourgeois allies against an ancien régime, the American workers were confronted with "bourgeois" attempts to further curb their impact on centers of power.

The view of the state as an agent of democratic reform was symbolized for American workers by what seemed an increasingly unrestricted white-male franchise. The nineteenth-century Golden Era of popular politics is enshrined as a period of unprecedented levels of (white-male) participation, where electoral mobilizations witnessed the introduction of economic demands. Yet this anchor of Lockian liberalism in America—the franchise—was, in Federalist fashion, weakened in response to the emerging factious spirit based on class. Resultant restrictions on working-class access, in combination with violent repression, diffused the impact of socialism on ideological and institutional centers of power in America. However, that same history shaped the institutional *and* ideological repertoires of the Populist and Progressive movements that followed. The surges of the nineteenth-century working class movement and the reprisals that followed tell that story.

Mike Davis contends that three major periods of working-class assertion, followed by dispersed political momentum, are evident in the nineteenth and early twentieth centuries: the early struggle for trade union
rights and a shorter working day (1832–1860); the post–Civil War out-
breaks of 1877, 1884–1887, and 1892–1896; and the waves of strikes
between 1909 and 1922.[27] Each of these periods bears witness to institutional responses seeking to limit the impact of the economically marginalized in American politics. These periods also correspond to the emergence of the Populist and Progressive movements and frame the dialogue
among all three movements. Each period also reflects state concessions
that dilute the concerns raised by the movements while simultaneously
adapting institutional constraints on popular sovereignty. These dialogues
and institutional developments, I contend, constitute the repertoires of action and ideology that underpin the social movements of the 1960s and,
ultimately, today.

During the first period of organized working-class politics
(1832–1860), a period also known as the "Golden Era" of political participation, faith in the franchise was high among white men. Piven and
Cloward report on the early ups and downs:

> [Voting levels] changed with the election of 1828, when turnout began a
> steady upward swing, reaching 80 percent of the eligible electorate in the
> presidential election of 1840. Turnout continued high in the second half of
> the nineteenth century, ranging from a low of about 69 percent in the presi-
> dential election of 1852, just before the electoral realignment that preceded
> the Civil War, to 82 and 83 percent respectively in the elections of 1860 and
> 1876.[28]

With the election of Andrew Jackson in 1828, the promise of the franchise gained greater legitimacy following the elimination of literacy, religious, and property qualifications. The appeal of Jacksonian democracy,
its impulse toward the masses, and its anti-monopoly ethos appealed to
the capitalist farmer and the entrepreneurial spirit of the petit-bourgeois
alike. Correspondingly, the openings permitted by the extended franchise
gave expression to organized working-class interests as witnessed by the
electoral showings of the Workingman's Parties of the same period. But
the lure of the Lockian liberal view, with its veil of consensus, propped up
as it was by Jackson's success, diverted the egalitarian appeal of the
working-class movements into a more legitimate analog. In addition, the

patronage party system effectively acted to integrate potential members of the working-class movements into nonsocialist orientations, especially among the waves of working-class immigrants by mid-century. Piven and Cloward note that "the era after 1830 in which party organization flourished was also an era in which the number of government jobs expanded."[29] The consolidation of both the Democratic and Whig (and then Republican) parties at the national level down to the precinct level substantially eclipsed other party efforts. The electoral arrangements unleashed in the Jacksonian period testify to the diffusing effect that a majoritarian system and party patronage (in an era of high voter turnout and rising economic concerns) can have on the consolidation of working-class demands.

But the believability of the "born equal" inscription on American liberalism would not go unchallenged. The consensus of American liberalism would be questioned again following the Civil War—but this time the challenge was immanent, coming from American farmers around whom the Lockian ideal flourished. The rise of American Populism would occur alongside, and at times in dialogue with, a renewal in the working-class movement. This emergence of Populism and its dialogue with the working-class movement of the day would provoke fear among consolidating elites. That fear gave way to electoral "reforms" that resulted in substantial disenfranchisement of marginalized Americans. The institutional developments of this era embraced the Federalist fears of factions and mob rule. In addition, the roots of the Populist revolt, which were simultaneously radical and conservative, and Populism's dialogue with the working-class movement substantially shaped the ideological terrain upon which future social movements would stand.

POPULISM: EGALITARIANISM FOR THE PAST

Populism can generally be described as an ideology that ascribes wisdom and virtue to the "common people." Historically, Populism is associated with agrarian interests that became displaced as a result of the industrial revolution. In America, Populism's more formal emergence as a social movement in the post–Civil War era signaled yet another challenge to the ideological and institutional advantages afforded organized elites over less-advantaged sectors of American society. Populism's thwarted challenge to American ideology and institutional arrangements testifies to the limited strategies and outcomes inherent in the American system. In addition, its history highlights the ability of the system to institutionally adapt to social movement success in such a way as to preserve both the veil of Lockian liberalism and the diffusion of interest endemic to the original Federalist design.

In his important work on American Populism, *Democratic Promise*, Lawrence Goodwyn observes that the Civil War had essentially changed everything in America. Dramatic realignments in party membership occurred beginning in the post–Reconstruction period as a focus on the new era of finance capital captured the attention of both the Republican and Democratic parties. Republican Party loyalties of northern and southern black Americans became irrelevant as the hopes for a reconstructed South dwindled. For its part, the Democratic Party began to abandon the cause of farmers in favor of new industry. As Goodwyn observes: "Everywhere—North and South, among Republicans and Democrats—business and financial entrepreneurs had achieved effective control of a restructured American party system."[30] In a reshaping of the Jeffersonian and Jacksonian tradition, the nation's farmers soon found that the economic system was not working in their favor; what's more, the political system was unresponsive to their dilemma.

Agricultural America saw itself at the center of the late-nineteenth-century universe; they were convinced, as Theodore Saloutos asserts, that "the fortunes of America weighed heavily on the fortunes of the farmers. As the farmers went so did the rest of the country."[31] A sense of abandonment and increasing irrelevance began to undermine the farmers' faith in the Lockian liberal premise that democracy and capitalism were simultaneous harvests. But essentially it was that faith in the Lockian universe—a universe replete with political equality, unlimited economic growth, and burgeoning agricultural entrepreneurship—that grounded their rebellion. That faith would gnaw at their alliance with labor, make them susceptible to Democratic Party co-optation, and eventually leave them diffused in the post–1896 electoral scheme.

Piven and Cloward observe that in the years following the Civil War, "rapid economic growth combined with extreme market instability and the predatory policies of bankers and corporations to promote the rise of popular protests over economic issues."[32] By the 1870s, farmers' movements cropped up in the Midwest and the South, fighting the railroad's high shipping rates and challenging "hard-money" monetary policies that increased farmers' indebtedness. Various movements of agrarian radicals—the Grangers, the Greenbacks, the Farmer's Alliances—emerged as the foundation for the populist movement whose agenda attacked the effects of industrialism. Populism opposed national banks and supported an expanded currency. It supported government regulation of the transportation and communication industries, progressive taxation, and federal subsidies for farming cooperatives. Eschewing politics, the early populist tendency was to cooperate on strengthening farmers' economic position through the establishment of farmers' cooperatives. But as these strategies waned in the late 1880s, the populist movement turned to electoral politics, often in alliance with working-class organizations like the Knights of Labor (a dialogue that began with the severe depression of 1873 when the Greenbackers and labor collaborated). And while the People's Party, which was forged in 1892 from the notion that "only when the forces of agriculture and labor were aligned into an effective political party could the interests of the farmers and labor be protected,"[33] did indeed make headway in the election of 1892, it did so despite fundamentally incongruous philosophies in a land that would not accommodate the interests of either group.

Populism and socialism each ran counter to the ideological and institutional conventions in American life. Moreover, the jerry-rigged marriage, based on anti-monopolism, was easily weakened by the populist alliance with the Democratic Party in 1896. The candidate that year, William Jennings Bryant, co-opted the rhetoric and issues of the third-party effort and was endorsed by the Populist Party by way of a fusion ticket. Bryant's own oratory shows the limits of radicalism in the land of Locke. The populist cries against big business, now at home in the Democratic platform, demonstrate the contradictions:

> I know the feelings of young men, and I know what it is to have a condition in our political society that makes it difficult for a young man to rise in life. . . . I want our government maintained as the fathers intended it. I want it so that [if a young man] enters politics he will not find arrayed against him all the great financial influences of society unless he is willing to join them and conspire against the welfare of the people as a whole. If he enters business I want him to be able to stand upon his own merits and not stand always in fear that some great trust will run him out of business.[34]

While elites of the era were made nervous by the energy the populists brought to the Democratic candidacy, in actuality that energy was dissipated substantially by the move. The difficulties that a majoritarian, two-party system present to third-party efforts were already obvious to both the working-class and farmers movements. But the move into the Democratic Party concealed an even more fundamental contradiction: socialism and Populism in America were asserting demands that extended far beyond the ideological boundaries of Lockian liberalism. A loss of faith in the unanimity of status and rights by the American farmers of the mid- and late-nineteenth century caused them to demand unanimity in a way that could not be accommodated under reigning capitalist economic arrangements.

Socialism in America, floundering as it was without an ancien régime, sought refuge in Populist alliances that had very different concerns at heart. These concerns, while more homegrown, would find little resonance in a nation that had trouble recognizing its own class character. One looking forward, one looking back, socialism and Populism were movements questioning the industrial shakedowns that jarred the Lockian liberal picaresque. While each movement reflected the contradiction between politics and economics inherent in American liberalism (and that being the source of their ideological discord with America), they did so from very different places. Theodore Saloutos comments:

> The attempt to view Populism through the eyes of the radical industrial workers of the East and Europe, instead of through the eyes of the disconsolate American farmers of the Middle West, Southwest, and South is tempting, but it is also misleading. To the more radical industrial elements, Marxism and Populism might have meant the alienation of man from his product, but to the agrarian populist it was largely alienation from his land, his equipment, his animals, and his personal belongings that made it difficult for him to raise a good crop, market it at a profit, sustain his family, educate his children, and discharge his obligations. . . . The farmers might have felt sorry for the workers being exploited by the large corporations, but they also viewed themselves as being a cut or two above the wage earners.[35]

If Populism and socialism made strange bedfellows, it is only because they were American that they shared the same bed at all. Their alliance, while practical in many respects, demonstrated the relative weakness of each in relation to the dominant national context. And all this was in an era of unprecedented electoral participation.

In the Jacksonian period preceding the Civil War, the white-male franchise was extended as property qualifications were all but eliminated across the country. The "era of the common man" signaled a defeat, in substantial measure, of the Federalist philosophy. With the end of the Civil War, the enfranchisement of newly freed slaves in the South, and European (working-class) immigrants in the North, proved to reinvent elite anxieties over majoritarian impulses. *Reinvent* is an appropriate word as so much had changed, both economically and sociologically, in American society after the war.

As a period characterized by party machines and corruption in the North (which Piven and Cloward term tribalism and clientelism), it was, nonetheless, also an era of unmatched black representation in the South, unparalleled voter turnout nationwide, and the ascendance of economic issues in political arenas prompted by both the Populist and working-class movements. The realignments in the two major parties, based in regional (North or South) hegemony, lowered competition for voters. The economic climate demanded that the newly realigned parties shift focus to big-business interests. By 1896, the era of the common man was but a memory in the wake of electorally engineered disenfranchisement. Historian Richard McCormick suggests that the late-nineteenth-century movements provoked public policy aimed at restricting the franchise:

Southern blacks and poor whites, by participating in the Populist movement, and new immigrants, by supporting the most corrupt city machines and flirting with socialism, convinced elites everywhere that unlimited suffrage fueled disorder. Under the banner of "reform," they enacted registration requirements, ballot laws, and other measures to restrict suffrage.[36]

The impact of socialism and Populism in America can be seen in the reactions they provoked. The restrictions on popular sovereignty that ensued, while paranoid in many respects, indicate the particular sensitivity that exists in America to the political expression of economic demands. The peculiar alliance between socialism and Populism did raise those issues. However, the alliance was unsustained by any coherent ideological critique, partly because of the incongruence of the two movements and partly because of each movement's failure to thematize the institutional limits of liberalism in America—and thus make strategic choices in relation to these limits.

Instead, Lockian liberalism was actively dictating its strategies and even movement alliances. As such, the issues raised, while radical in their attack on finance capital, were ultimately translatable into Democratic

Party parlance. Populism was thus disarmed by both ideological co-optation as well as party/electoral mechanisms. In attempting to weigh the interests of farmers and immigrant workers *and* emerging businesses, the Democratic Party adopted rhetorical attacks on monopolies but curbed demands. Bryan's defeat in 1896 indicates the limited viability of an even watered-down version of anti-business rhetoric in a political climate increasingly dominated, ideologically and institutionally, by industrial interests. Evidence of the twin demands of an increasingly centralized economy and the state's need to develop the administrative capacity for its management and direction are already present.

American social movements were confronted with new and more pernicious adaptations of traditional constraints. The difficulty labor Populism experienced in establishing an ideologically unifying framework was not just a problem of thinking through the competing agrarian–industrial interests. Both political diffusion and the lack of ideological consistency fed off each other under the assault of an increasingly complex and economically destabilizing context. The era of Progressive reform that followed the Populist–labor surge paradoxically captures, in movement form, the emerging systemic demands of modernization in the American institutional context.

The success of the Progressive movement led to sharp decreases in voting participation. Ideologically speaking, Progressivism served as a rhetorical nod to the diluted messages of socialism and Populism, but it did so in a way that fundamentally eroded the few mechanisms of popular control available (and so necessary) to democratic social movements. In exactly the same time period that modernizing forces are bringing automation and administration into the economic and political realms full bloom, Progressivism weakens the levers of accountability. Ironically, Progressivism as a social movement expresses the repressed concern for the have-nots, but in perhaps the only acceptable format possible in America: without their control and participation. Progressivism, in this sense, represents the ideological and institutional bias of the American system internalized in a social movement form.

In so doing, the Progressive movement shored up certain elements of the Lockian liberal ideology while it took its cues, so to speak, from the Federalists. With a wink and a kind word, Progressivism sought to limit the political participation of lower-income citizens while it promoted the role of government in protecting citizens from unregulated capital. Symbolically embracing the spirit of egalitarianism in the movements of workers and farmers, Progressivism encouraged the separation of ends from means, and in so doing, undermined the substantive quality of the ends.

Social reforms without mechanisms of accountability, it can be argued, are better than no reforms at all. This is the spirit of Progressivism, which in many respects is echoed in the New Deal. In both the Progressive and New Deal eras, genuine gains were made meeting the needs of not only the most exploited segments of American society but stabilizing a marginal middle class as well. However, the expansion of constraints on popular control that accompanied those gains, more than simply the expanded role of the state, encouraged a fragmentation of political interests that further crippled the full impact of social movements in American politics. In both cases, agitation from below instigated concessions from above. But those concessions were accompanied by institutional developments that undermined the possibility of social movements gaining coherent electoral expression. Two mitigating factors—the born equal doctrine of Lockian liberalism shored up in the Progressive era, and accompanying electoral demobilization—constrained social movements from advancing a coherent ideological critique and from consolidating political power.

In the years of the Great Depression, these two inheritances from the Progressive era led interests such as labor, African Americans, the unemployed, and the homeless to mobilize in isolated and often inchoate ways. And while much of the New Deal is indeed a response to the threat of this mass dislocation, and significant reforms were made, the ensuing institutional arrangements (referred to here by Theodore Lowi's term, interest-group liberalism) channeled social movements into an individuated and directly clientelist relationship with the state that bypassed the question of electoral arrangements, upon which so much of the fate of social movements depends. The ideological counterpart, pluralism, rationalized single-issue organizing among social movements and cloaked the inequality of group politics. As such, the social benefits of the New Deal, significant as they were, were also accompanied by a political structure that undermined future social movement coherence and impact.

PROGRESSIVISM: A LIBERAL FUTURE WITHOUT RABBLE

One consequence of the election of 1896 was the demobilization of the electorate through a series of electoral contrivances aimed at limiting the franchise of southern blacks, northern working-class immigrants, and poor white tenant farmers. Registration qualifications such as literacy tests and poll taxes, reapportionment schemes, and balloting reforms rationalized the sectional balance of power that Goodwyn calls the Republican Party's big monopoly in the North and the Democratic Party's little monopoly in the South. Big-business influence nationally and rabble-rousing from below provoked electoral restriction and secured the trend of noncompetitive parties. As evidence of the effectiveness of these electoral schemes, voter turnout for presidential elections between 1840 and 1896 would range from 69 percent to 83 percent; by 1924 voter turnout had steadily declined to just 49 percent.[37] Piven and Cloward contend:

> As the possibilities of popular electoral mobilizations began to threaten the interests of ruling groups in the late-nineteenth-century United States, they responded by sponsoring something like a democratic counter-revolution. A series of "reforms" were introduced which weakened the ability of local parties to maintain high participation among lower-strata voters, and which impeded voting by lower-strata people. The effect of these changes was to marginalize potentially contentious groups away from the electoral system.[38]

But the social movement protests of workers and farmers that began after the Civil War did not come to an end with efforts to restrict the franchise. The economic conditions at the turn of the century brought on intense waves of strikes, a reinvigorated farmers' movement, and a host of reformist campaigns for the protection of children, women, slum dwellers, and consumers. The women's suffrage movement increased in steam and made headway during this period, and by 1920 women gained the right to vote. The first nationally organized, black-led efforts to fight segregation, lynching, and race riots also appeared at this time. The American working-class movement entered its most contradictory phase, illustrated by the heightened polarization between trade unionism under Samuel Gompers of the American Federation of Labor and the more political and unifying aims of Eugene Debs. In his presidential bid as the Socialist Party candidate in 1912, Debs won almost 900,000 votes, capturing an unprecedented 6 percent of the vote.

The period between 1901 and 1921 was also, and perhaps fundamentally, a period of intense concentration of capital into the hands of powerful corporations; Howard Zinn observes that "by 1904, 318 trusts, with capital of more than seven billion dollars, controlled 40 percent of the U.S. manufacturing."[39] The dominance of business in American affairs occurred alongside pestilent and deteriorating conditions in the cities among the unskilled working class and general social decline among marginal sectors. The economic panic of 1907, the waves of strikes, and the rise in demands for protective legislation exerted pressure on the two major parties.

What ultimately gave this era its name was not the unrest that raised the issues. In large part, Progressivism and the short-lived party that bore its name were the result of powerful elites making limited concessions to reform-minded Americans in an effort to stabilize the economic system in a time of uncertainty. The Progressive Period, engineered under the presidencies of Taft, Theodore Roosevelt, and Wilson, marked an era that has been characterized as "a conscious and successful effort to guide and control the economic and social policies of federal, state, and municipal government by various business groupings in their own long-range interest."[40] Inspired by Federalist-like notions of efficiency and stability, the Progressive era witnessed a slew of legislation aimed at ameliorating the most severe abuses of the economy, bringing business under the control of the state:

> Under Theodore Roosevelt there was the Meat Inspection Act, the Hepburn Act to regulate the railroads and pipelines, a Pure Food and Drug Act. Under Taft, the Mann–Elkins Act put telephone and telegraph systems under the regulation of the Interstate Commerce Commission. In Woodrow Wilson's presidency, the Federal Trade Commission was introduced to control the growth of monopolies, and the Federal Reserve Act to regulate the country's money and banking system. Under Taft were proposed the Sixteenth Amendment to the Constitution, allowing a graduated income tax, and the Seventeenth Amendment, providing for election of Senators directly by popular vote.[41]

These gains were real indeed. But the ideological justifications and the institutional results of the Progressive era were in fact typically American, and therefore, the gains were limited by a new version of Lockian liberalism and new restraints on popular control. In this period there was a major political shift that would later shape the New Deal and the institutionalization of interest-group liberalism. The Progressive era was the beginning of the deceptive appearance of social reforms delivered in a form that in fact prohibited the instigating movement from gaining coherent formal expression, and, at the same time, undercut the mechanisms for democratic expression of group interest.

During the Progressive era, authentic government regulation of industry began. But this seemingly social function developed alongside electoral reform and had the effect of detaching the electorate from newly formed government agencies. As party competition and membership declined at the beginning of the twentieth century, newly organized interests sought, and in many instances gained, a foothold in American politics. Richard McCormick, in his book *From Realignment to Reform*, observes:

> The first fifteen years of the twentieth century . . . more precisely, the brief period from 1904 to 1908 saw a remarkable compressed political transformation. During these years the regulatory revolution peaked; new and powerful agencies of government came into being everywhere. At the same time voter turnout declined, ticket splitting increased, and organized social, economic, and reform-minded groups began to exercise power more systematically than before.[42]

The diminishing of electoral mechanisms of accountability in the policy-making process is not, as I have asserted elsewhere, a necessary outcome of government growth and regulation; however, the degree to which such a tendency can even be said to exist is certainly compounded, if not created, in a political atmosphere of electoral decline. As a result, a dangerous precedent is established in the Progressive era that substitutes the symbolic representation of organized interest for the electoral mandate required of parties (a type of liberal Leninism, if you will). Even though third-party efforts have been substantially hindered since the Founding, the Progressive era further hindered the interests of the poor and marginalized in America from democratic expression and accountability. The more egalitarian-minded groups of the Progressive era took gains where they could find them, however, not in a form that would politically empower those whom they claimed to represent. The justification for this substitution of groups for parties in representing interest had its roots in the academy. The scientific faith in efficiency proliferated under industrial capitalism and shaped the Progressive era's emphasis on the stabilization and rationalization of social crises. The name itself reflects its teleological point of view: any problem or crisis could, and would, be brought under control and managed rationally. As such, the state becomes a site for group management, divorced from the messy business of parties, conflict, and accountability.

The academic counterpart to the Progressive era's political developments can be found in the theory of pluralism, first advanced by Arthur Bentley in his 1908 book *Governmental Processes*. There he contends that the unit of analysis in political science should be the group. Eschewing normative concepts like the common good or public interest, Bentley suggested that countervailing groups produce society and that universalistic pretensions conceal the real character of the nation–state. Group competition, therefore, becomes the regulating principle. Parties, in Bentley's view, stifle group competition with their mission to aggregate groups and present unifying platforms. Bentley's pluralist model internalizes the competition premises of free-market capitalism. It assumes that group formation is "automatic," much like Locke, Jefferson, and Adam Smith saw democracy as reflected in market ideals. As such, pluralism and Progressivism reveal a renewed faith in Lockian liberalism. Progressivism's red herring is that it attempts to regulate the market and protect the poor, but, in Bentlian terms, these concessions can be seen as bargains reached between groups.

While Bentley's work in many ways opened the door to seeing that politics, conflicts, and bargaining are the "stuff" that politics is made of, it rationalizes that such notions exist in lieu of mechanisms of accountability (i.e., strong parties) that might uphold some greater normative interest, such as democracy itself. In effect, pluralism, in its Progressive era incarnation, justified the political shifts in post–1896 America. The reforms of that era, while real and beneficial in many respects, reflect the national acquiescence to Lockian liberalism and epitomize the particular tendency of the American system to absorb and dilute ideological challenges from the Left and adapt its institutional arrangements in ways that diminish the impact of future social movement advances.

The consequences of the Progressive era have contributed contradictory elements to the repertoires of ideology and action available to social movements today. Progressivism established that social movements have indeed influenced policies. However, it is not readily perceived that the social movement influence of the era was the result of momentum built up during the years when the franchise was less restricted. The era also reveals that the concessions that were, in some measure, a response to a franchise-driven threat, were ultimately defined by the interests of liberal capitalism and not by the movements themselves. Ultimately, Progressivism's concessions, granted in an atmosphere of declining electoral influence, contribute the false impression to social movement thinking that non-electorally based group politics is an effective format for democratic social movements.

During the Progressive era, national government became an instrument for social movement reforms, but only in symbolic and diluted ways. Not only was the content of the various movements' demands undermined, but, and perhaps more importantly, the mechanisms for consent were further limited.

An additional consequence of the period is the ideological swirl that Progressivism makes of socialism, Populism, and Lockian liberalism for the twentieth century. Indeed, Progressivism, backed by the articulatory power of the state, effectively obscured the distinctive features of socialism and Populism (which later becomes a problem for social movements of the sixties) and overcame each in its reassertion of liberal capitalism. But even more than a defeat for Populism, which after all had at heart a Lockian world view, Progressivism dealt a heavy blow to socialism in America. Louis Hartz suggests:

> One can use the term "Liberal Reform" to describe the Western movement which emerged toward the end of the nineteenth century to adapt a classical liberalism to the purposes of small propertied interests and the laboring class and at the same time which rejected socialism. But the American movement, now as during that age itself, was in a unique position. For swallowing up both peasantry and proletariat into the "petit-bourgeois" scheme, America created two universal effects. It prevented socialism from challenging its Liberal Reform in any effective way, and at the same time it enslaved its Liberal Reform to the [Horatio] Alger dream of democratic capitalism.[43]

The ideological and electoral adaptations that became a central fact of American life during the Progressive period persisted through the New Deal era, with modifications. Those modifications are in large part due to the reactivation of northern working-class voters recruited by the Democratic Party during the New Deal years. The New Deal Coalition under Franklin Delano Roosevelt (FDR) was responsible for a realignment of the two major parties. That realignment was the result of the Democratic alliance between northern urban workers and traditional white southern Democrats. Brought on by the economic and social crisis of the Great Depression, FDR reinvigorated the old party machines of the urban North (machines that prompted Progressive "reform") and strengthened ties to labor unions in an effort to sustain an electoral base. Unwilling to challenge the segregationist southern Democrats, FDR left the crippled black franchise as it was. The coalition, engineered by FDR to support New Deal policies, required only limited remobilization of the franchise that had been contracted by the system of 1896.

Like the movements that responded to the panic of 1907, the working-class movements and other reform movements of the Great Depression era were galvanized by the economic collapse of 1929. The combined effect of increased protest and a partially widened franchise supported increases in electoral turnout and helped shape the direction of New Deal programs.[44] In 1936, voter turnout rose to 57 percent and to a high of 62 percent in 1940. But in large part, the electoral possibilities of movements of the New Deal era remained constrained not only by the preserved elements of the system of 1896, but by reinvented liberal constraints sanctioned by pluralist notions of representation. While the relief and employment programs of the New Deal were in part major concessions to the mobilizations of marginalized people, the institutional developments in the Executive Branch did not encourage the electoral and self-governing strength of those constituencies. Indeed, given the established constraints of the system, New Deal developments ultimately proved to rationalize a system of representation that was becoming less and less dependent on electoral organization and more dependent on a corporate model of interest groups.

While significant expression of discontents both shaped and were later further unleashed by the early American adaptation of the Keynesian welfare state,[45] its meaning is a mixed one for social movements today. The New Deal's most experimental programs and its rhetorical and sentimental edge initially inspired, in Richard Hofstadter's words:

a kind of pervasive tenderness for the underdog, for the Okies, the share-croppers, the characters in John Steinbeck's novels, the subjects who posed for the FSA photographers, for what were called, until a revulsion set in, "the little people."[46]

Indeed, the development of the welfare state in America initially evidenced an exceptional level of commitment not only to America's most impoverished, such as expressed in the first Aid to Dependent Families legislation of 1941[47] and the enactment of Social Security in 1935, but in the federal support for the arts and letters as well. Indeed, it would be just such "tenderness," coupled with Roosevelt's administrative lead, that led conservative critics to brand it Communist. Not withstanding the strains the incipient Cold War wrought upon Americans mobilized under the rising expectations of federal programs and the anticipated openings for American labor, the New Deal itself undermined their potential. Indeed, the complex relations that begin in this era represent the core issues confronting democratic social movements today. While the systemic demands of international capitalism and its administration brought forth, for practical capitalist reasons, the Keynesian welfare state, its political mediation remains a matter of some latitude. As a result, whereas welfare proved fundamental to the survival of hundreds of thousands of Americans over the last sixty-five years, and today can be shown to be essential to the interests of "new" social movements, the attendant administrative growth in a context of vanishing political accountability necessarily threatens the efforts and effects intended.

In America, the welfare state was erected upon the "liberal" exclusions of two hundred years. The complexity of state functions and modern life overwhelm the already exclusive two parties; the growth of administrative state apparatus calls upon specialized constituencies—expert, scientific, organized. The party function further weakens in a country of weak parties. Consequently, as the few democratic controls available begin to weaken, the electoral arena, as compared with many European democracies, becomes overwhelmed by the economic imperatives and administrative developments that increasingly elude the grasp of viable publics. Unresponsive parties and bureaucracies widen the gap between discontent and "legitimate" channels.

Movements in the post–World War II era, confronted with the rise of interest-group liberalism and all its attendant institutional and ideological features, applied and combined the inherited repertoires of ideologies and practices in new and provocative ways. The struggle for civil rights, an invigorated youth movement—particularly around opposition to the Vietnam War—and the emergent women's movement all testified to a new wave of social movement activity that distinguished itself from its state-oriented predecessors. Couching themselves in new variants of socialism, Populism, and Progressivism, the New Left, or New Politics, as it was variously labeled, signaled new developments in the focus, forms, and aims of American social movements. Their ideological orientations tended to justify, even require, a shift toward a more symbolic politic.

In the next chapter, I will suggest that developments in American social movement ideologies and practices in the 1960s were built upon the exclusions and defeats of movements before them. Importantly, the post–

New Deal context presented the movements of the 1960s with new barriers to legitimate access to formal processes. New institutional barriers to mass-based democratic movements, such as interest-group politicking at the Executive Branch level and the increasingly corporate structure of the Democratic and Republican parties, combined with historical obstacles to produce "new" responses on the part of social movements. As a result, social movements in this era became increasingly reliant on symbolic politics, both ideologically and practically. Out of the disapproving dialectic of the American state and the movements before them, *new* social movements are born.

NOTES

1. Louis Hartz, *The Liberal Tradition in America* (New York: Harcourt Brace and World, 1955), p. 44.

2. As formulated by Theodore Lowi, *The End of Liberalism: The Second Republic of the United States* (New York: W. W. Norton & Co., 1979, 1969). For my argument regarding the role of social movements in relation to interest-group liberalism, see chapter 4, "Interest-Group Liberalism and the Rise of Cultural Politics: Strategy v. Identity."

3. Hartz, p. 11.

4. See Werner Sombart, *Why Is There No Socialism in America?* edited by C. T. Husbands (White Plains, N.Y.: M.E. Sharpe, 1976).

5. See Mike Davis, *Prisoners of the American Dream* (London: Verso, 1986).

6. See Selig Pearlman's *A Theory of the Labor Movement* (New York: Macmillan, 1928), and for a lively discussion of various theories of "American exceptionalism," see John Laslet and Seymour Martin Lipsett's edited collection of essays (with comment and author reply) on the subject in *Failure of a Dream? Essays in the History of American Socialism* (Berkeley: University of California Press, 1984, 1974).

7. John Patrick Digging, "Knowledge and Sorrow: Louis Hartz's Quarrel with American History," in *Political Theory*, vol. 16, n. 3 (1988), p. 360.

8. Hartz, p. 41.

9. Hartz, p. 9.

10. Joseph Ellis, *American Sphinx* (New York: Knopf, 1997), p. 59.

11. Ibid., p. 56.

12. From chapter 10 excerpt of Charles Beard's *The Economic Basis of Politics and Related Writings* (New York: Vintage Books, 1975), reprinted in *American Government: Readings and Cases* (New York: HarperCollins, 1993), pp. 33–43.

13. Hartz, p. 79.

14. James Madison, "No. 10," *The Federalist Papers*, edited by Isaac Kramnick (London: Penguin Books, 1987), p. 123.

15. Ibid., p. 124.

16. Frances Fox Piven and Richard Cloward, *Why Americans Don't Vote* (New York: Pantheon, 1988), p. 26.

17. Hartz, p. 114.

18. The speech appears in *The Debate of the State Conventions on the Adoption of the Federal Constitution, As Recommended by the General Convention at Philadelphia in 1787*, J. Elliot, ed. (Philadelphia, 1866), sect II, 301.

19. Diggins, p. 362.

20. Quoted in Joseph Ellis, *American Sphinx*, p. 100.

21. Hartz, pp. 85–86.

22. Hartz, p. 86.

23. Mike Davis, *Prisoners of the American Dream* (London: Verso Press, 1986), p. 13.

24. Nathan Fine, *Labor and Farmer Parties in the United States, 1828–1928* (New York: Rand School of Social Science, 1928), pp. 13–14.

25. Again, see *Failure of a Dream.*

26. Davis, pp. 18–19.

27. Davis, p. 17.

28. Piven and Cloward, *Why Americans Don't Vote*, p. 29.

29. Piven and Cloward, *Why Americans Don't Vote*, p. 37.

30. Lawrence Goodwyn, *The Populist Movement* (London: Oxford University Press, 1980, 1978), p. 7. Note that this reprint is an abridged edition of *Democratic Promise* (London: Oxford University Press, 1978).

31. Theodore Saloutos, "Radicalism and the Agrarian Tradition: Reply," in *Failure of a Dream?* p. 75.

32. Piven and Cloward, *Why Americans Don't Vote*, p. 41.

33. Theodore Saloutos, "Radicalism and the Agrarian Tradition," in *Failure of a Dream?* p. 54.

34. In Eric Goldman, *A Rendezvous with Destiny: A History of Modern American Reform* (New York: Vintage Books, 1977, 1956), pp. 50–51.

35. Ibid., pp. 60–61.

36. Richard P. McCormick, "The Party Period and Public Policy: An Exploratory Hypothesis," in *Journal of American History*, vol. 66 (1979), p. 295.

37. See Piven and Cloward, *Why Americans Don't Vote*, chapter 2.

38. Ibid., p. 27.

39. Howard Zinn, *A People's History of the United States* (New York: Harper Collins, 1980), pp. 342–343.

40. See James Weinstein, *The Corporate Ideal in the Liberal State: 1900–1918* (Boston: Beacon Press, 1969).

41. Zinn, p. 341.

42. Richard McCormick, *From Realignment to Reform: Political Change in New York State, 1893–1910* (Ithaca, N.Y.: Cornell University Press, 1981), p. 271.

43. Hartz, p. 228.

44. For a full discussion of the relationship between protest, electoral shifts, and the economic climate of the 1930s, see Piven and Cloward, *Poor People's Movements* (New York: Vintage Books, 1977).

45. See Frances Fox Piven and Richard Cloward, *Poor People's Movements: Why They Succeed, How They Fail* (New York: Pantheon Books, 1977).

46. Richard Hofstadter, *The Age of Reform* (New York: Knopf, 1955), p. 324.

Chapter Four

Interest-Group Liberalism and the Rise of Cultural Politics: Strategy v. Identity

Precision was sacrificed for a greater degree of suggestion.

Abbie Hoffman on Chicago, 1968

While 1968 can arguably be called the symbolic birth year of NSMs, the eruptions of that year, both in Europe and the United States, can be traced in part to developments in state administration functions associated with the Keynesian welfare state. At the same time, whereas 1968 was in many respects a global phenomenon,[1] the intensity with which U.S. social movements took the "cultural turn" can best be understood in relation to historical exclusions recast under the pressures of new macro developments and the post–New Deal institutional context. While the growth of the administrative state and instrumental logics are the backdrop to the 1960s' drop-out, radical U.S. social movements in large part chose the path of symbolic politics in response to a narrow two-party system and the rise of interest-group liberalism. In this sense, the cultural turn can be seen as a pragmatic yet ultimately baffling attempt to retain a radical posture in an otherwise deradicalizing context.

Unfortunately, the new posture, especially in the American context, could not provide a sustainable politic related to the demands sought. Eventually, the new movements moved along one of two resulting trajectories: integration into the orbit of interest-group politics or symbolic radicalism ending in collapse. This bifurcated pattern has its roots in the early Civil Rights movement where, at least until approximately 1966, combined strategic and symbolic modes coexisted. At that time, the movement began suffering from the disorganizing effects of co-optation, on the one hand,

and the heightened rhetoric of symbolic militancy, on the other. These effects were evident as well in two other major movements of those years: the anti-Vietnam War movement and the women's movement. After 1967, the desire for and legitimacy of combining institutional approaches with radical politics wanes. Despite Martin Luther King's efforts after 1967 to re-combine radicalism and strategic action through the Poor People's Movement, the tradition was essentially submerged after his assassination. Whereas what are later to be dubbed the NSMs embrace the turn away from the state, thus conceding institutional influence to, in the best case, liberal interest groups, they discover themselves unable to develop a sustainable politic. Integration or collapse become predictable outcomes.

The choices made by the social movements of the 1960s can be grasped in exemplary "moments"[2] that reveal the complex of ideological, institutional, and economic constraints that informed those choices. Illustrative examples can be drawn from the Civil Rights, anti-Vietnam War, and women's movements, which help to clarify the contradictory legacy the 1960s made available to current social movements—a legacy, I'll argue, that in many respects is uniquely American.

The developments in movement repertoires emerging from the social movements of the 1960s gave emphasis to three features: a contradictory stance toward the state that evidences itself in an anti-statist, anti-bureaucratic politic alongside the seeking of constitutional protections as well as resources from the state; a concern with the prefigurative, which manifests itself as the demand for adherence to highly egalitarian social norms and organizational structures that prove to be shifting, indeterminate, and unaccountable; and the replacement of an untenable Marxist teleological theory with a politics of identity that ultimately reduces questions of economics, politics, and ideology to cultural struggles based on experience and location. I do not agree with NSM theorists who suggest that the new emphasis on "autonomy and identity (with their organizational correlates such as decentralization, self-government, and self-help) and opposition to manipulation, control, dependence, bureaucratization, and regulation"[3] are significantly contestational. The three trends stipulated above, I'll argue in the next chapter, define and hamper progressive social movements in the United States today.

Within the American context, the fluidity and decentralized social movement form celebrated by NSM theory can also be seen as a reflection of the intentional fragmentation of organized interest generated by U.S. institutional arrangements. Here it can be said that social movements have internalized the ideological limits of Lockian liberalism in an era of interest-group pluralism. As a reflection of these constraints, NSMs indicate a lack of critical distance from the context in which they are enmeshed. As a result, these movements fall prey to either the integrating and deradicalizing force of interest-group politics or to a cycle of exacting internal demands and self-immolation. Unlocking the logic of interest-group liberalism and attendant political patterns helps clarify the pressures of the American context on social movements after World War II.

Interest-group liberalism describes a post–New Deal political context characterized by three trends that negatively affect democratic accountability. Theodore Lowi argues that the new trends transform and further an already existing constraint on popular control. In the first case, interest-group liberalism is characterized by a decrease in the mechanisms of popular control, such as the well-documented decline of parties and voter-participation levels. Secondly, interest-group liberalism favors the maintenance of old and the creation of new structures of privilege. In this case, Lowi argues, the old class bias is translated into a bias favoring wealthy interest groups. Thirdly, he asserts that interest groups reinforce governmental resistance to change by insulating governments from popular checks of all kinds.

Interestingly, Lowi and many NSM theorists share some similar conclusions, albeit with different emphases and logics. For many of the NSM theorists, the rise of the Keynesian welfare state, while providing needed social services, has fostered a type of administrative rationality that has undermined political accountability and reinforced a policy bias toward organized elites.[4] Despite the fact that, except for a brief period of significant relief-giving, the U.S. welfare state has never matched the size or scope of its European counterparts, a similar critique is nestled in Lowi's work. One can imagine that the effects of modernization described by many NSM theorists would only be more severe in the absence of a system of proportional representation, and public limits on campaign financing are generally present.

Indeed, the rise of the administrative state in the United States occurred in a context where the labor movement and other significant challenges to the ideological, economic, and political dominance of the two major parties were already significantly integrated. In this sense, Lowi's concept of interest-group liberalism helps us elucidate how the systemic tendencies of the administrative state express themselves within the ideological traditions and institutional context of the United States. This helps us grasp the choices of the 1960s' social movements and the peculiarly American challenges facing contemporary U.S. social movements.

After the New Deal, social movements agitating for the expansion of democratic rights and economic justice faced a decision, consciously or unconsciously, to either reconstitute along interest-group lines or remain largely symbolic, and thus vulnerable to collapse. It is important to re-assert here that I am not arguing that the development of the welfare state as such is cause of the social movement form. I am arguing that the choices of U.S. social movements are framed by the bureaucratic state's development in a country that from its inception has seen parties (espe-cially those that challenge liberalism from the Left) as threats to be con-tained. Without diverse parties able to affect electoral accountability, plu-ralism remains yet another manifestation of a "marketplace" liberalism that eschews notions of popular control and economic justice.

Lowi has been a relentless critic of interest-group liberalism, which he describes as policy making without laws. Lowi's concerns were shaped by the pluralist paradigm he encountered while a student at Yale in the 1950s. The developments of pluralist theory and analysis, beginning with Bentley and extended by David Truman in his work *The Govern-mental Process* (1951), frame Lowi's arguments regarding the antide-mocratic character of interest-group politics. Lowi suggested that plu-ralism's descriptive claim was rationalizing the very developments in institutional arrangements, which he saw as contradictory to democratic government. Pluralist scholars, like David Truman, took as their starting point the sociology of society in an effort to look behind the unidimen-sional studies that emphasized formal institutions and constitutional comparisons. Truman posited that society's complex nature would auto-matically give rise to interest groups and that "serious" complaints would be addressed and corrected through the representation of interest groups. For Lowi, the inherent assumption of the pluralist model is that modernization inevitably brings with it administration dependent on in-terest-group representation. His greatest concern, expressed in virtually all his work, is that the legislative process, and the concomitant concern for justice under the rule of law, is being replaced by unequal bargain-ing. Unequal bargaining is reflected in the disproportionate influence that wealthy interest groups possess.[5]

In the policies and institutional developments of the New Deal, Lowi argues, legislative control shifted from elected representatives in Congress to agencies of the Executive Branch. These agencies dominate the policy process and stabilize relationships among themselves, pressure groups, and Congress through the development of "iron triangles," thus giving elites greater control over an increasingly unengaged electorate. Lowi, as an early critic of executive power and bureaucratic control of legislative detail, warns against congressional legislative abdication, the weakening of parties, low voter turnout, and the influence of interest groups that characterize the post–New Deal political terrain. His warnings reveal a normative concern with democratic governments' need for legitimating institutions that mitigate the influence of powerful elites. He argues:

> In whatever form and by whatever label, the purpose of representation and of reform in representation is the same: to deal with the problem of power—to bring the democratic spirit into some kind of psychological balance with the harsh realities of government coerciveness. The problem is that the new representation embodied in the broad notion of interest-group liberalism is a pathological adjustment to the problem. Interest-group liberal solutions to the problem of power provide the system with stability by spreading a sense of representation at the expense of genuine flexibility, at the expense of democratic forms, and ultimately at the expense of legitimacy.[6]

Lowi's observations contribute to an understanding of the institutional and ideological features of the American system after World War II.

In the post–New Deal climate, defined by electoral impediments, limited party competition, and clientelist agencies of the Executive Branch, most social movements became polarized between interest-group politics and a symbolic radicalism. Each tendency seemed unaware of the ideological and institutional constraints of their respective paths, or more importantly, what might be needed to overcome them. It is in this climate, I argue, that the characteristics associated with NSMs emerged. That is to say, NSMs are the social versions of the institutionalized interest group: each is the product of systemic trends associated with modernization and historical developments in the American post–New Deal context.

As discussed earlier, NSMs are concerned with preserving autonomy and identity against the encroachments of the state. NSMs, it follows, represent a withdrawal from the kind of combination strategy (both electoral and protest oriented) that largely came to an end following the decline of the early Civil Rights movement in the mid-1960s.[7] As argued in chapter 3, the institutional possibilities for successful social movement impact have historically been limited to moments when protest coincides with an unstable electoral climate, as in the early Civil Rights movement. But there too we see the consequence of success. While legislative gains were indeed obtained, the trajectories for social movements became misleadingly defined by the "two" faces of the Civil Rights movement: co-optation v. symbolic radicalism. Whereas the New Deal gains of the previous era period provided a rhetorical base from which to argue for the state's social and economic responsibilities, as was done by the early Civil Rights movement, ultimately it was a rhetoric unconnected to effective mechanisms of accountability.

Social movements, like the later Civil Rights movement, that adopted Executive Branch relations and congressional lobbying as a means of securing legislative aims did so at the expense of more far-reaching, systemic reforms (such as pushing King's economic agenda or rallying for electoral party reforms). In effect, the New Deal left social movements linked to strategies that are dependent on a sympathetic political climate, which, as we can see today, changes. This arrangement leaves democratic social movements particularly hard-pressed for institutional leverage of any kind.

The sense of loss that social movements experienced as their organizations underwent demobilization inspired a more insular, purist form of activity, which frequently bounced between extreme militancy and utopian communalism. Both the interest-group route and the radical route, ironically, evidence attachment to the group theory of politics, and neither offers a coherent alternative to the dominant paradigm or institutional arrangements.

Apart from the struggle for the expanded franchise, and other early Civil Rights campaigns that threatened to break up the Democratic Party electoral coalition built during the New Deal,[8] the social movements that followed were limited in their strategies due to their lack of institutional access or leverage. In the case of the voting-rights campaigns of the early and mid-sixties, the potential infusion of black voters into the Democratic Party caused alarm and concessions. The presence of new constituents within the party meant new demands that ran counter to the interests of one of the party's oldest sectors: white southerners. The very threat of an expanded franchise brought concessions but, as in the past, major party concessions diluted the social movement demands with the hope of stabilizing electoral patterns. In an effort to diffuse increasingly violent opposition to the dedicated Civil Rights movement in the South, President Kennedy sought to "channel" the Civil Rights movement into executive relations. It is also true that this was both beneficial and debilitating for the Civil Rights agenda.

The multi-pronged strategies of the Civil Rights movement testifies to the power of noninstitutional tactics in the context of electoral instability, which generates access. It was a turning point in American social movement history because the access gained drew much of its energy into the networks of interest-group liberalism. Those sectors and outgrowths of the Civil Rights movements that avoided the orbit of interest-group politics (among them segments of the Student Non-Violent Coordinating Committee [SNCC], the Black Panthers, and the Black Muslim community) engaged in various forms of militancy rooted in identity claims. Much of what occurred in the years after the major legislative victories of the Civil Rights movement, both in terms of movement stances and government repressions, has obscured the circumstances surrounding what can be loosely termed the "cultural turn."

While I am suggesting that the constraints that conditioned the choices and patterns of sixties social movements presented real obstacles to their success, I am not, however, suggesting that those constraints were determinant or irreversible. This raises the more general question as to the degree and type of agency social movements possess regarding the climate, both institutional and ideological, within which they operate. In part three I will return to this question from a theoretical perspective, but here I would like to suggest that key movements of the late sixties did not consider or continue strategies aimed at challenging electoral arrangements, in large part because of the limited success and diffusing effects such a strategy produced for the Civil Rights movement.

The bifurcation of movement repertoires is a reflection of both the historical limits of ideology and institutions in the American context, and the internalization of those limits in movement ideology itself. The social movements of the late sixties, in an effort to sustain their radical stance, shifted to symbolic or cultural grounds, abdicated the institutional realm, and developed ideologies that obscured the relation between symbolic and institutional politics. In other words, their cultural turn lacked a reflexive moment. As long as interest-group pluralism, with its ersatz forms of representation and legitimation, remained unchanged, the participatory impulse of democratic social movements would be, it seemed, consigned to a parallel type of symbolic group politics.

THE RISE OF CULTURAL POLITICS: THE ROOTS
OF NEW SOCIAL MOVEMENT IDEOLOGY

If we begin with Offe's definition of NSMs as rejecting institutional politics, we see that the early Civil Rights movement does not conform—it used electoral realignment along with mass mobilizations to momentarily crack the elite bias of interest-group liberalism. Unfortunately, significant elements (the National Association for the Advancement of Colored People [NAACP], for example) of the Civil Rights movement were absorbed by the Democratic Party in a way that the most egalitarian and democratizing impulses, represented by King's Southern Christian Leadership Council's (SCLC) economic proposals, were thwarted. The Civil Rights movement was not able to gain support within the Democratic Party for its emerging economic agenda (circa 1967). Already enmeshed in deals with the Democrat-controlled Executive Branch and Congress, Civil Rights leaders saw no opportunity to push for structural reform. Once in the party, their leverage was diminished.

In contrast to the institutional strategies of the early Civil Rights movement, social movements of the late 1960s are the first to have been identified by European theorists as exhibiting a new focus. The lessons of the Civil Rights movement led many social movements of the day to reject institutional strategies and rely on cultural strategies to retain a radical stance. In this regard, the focus, forms, and aims of social movements of the late 1960s define the context that continues to inform movements today.

In particular, the cultural turn that various movements took, primarily in the form of identity politics, stands in direct relation to the limited options available at the time. This cultural stance can be observed in social movement thinking today. Nonetheless, I contend that while explainable today, the context itself was not rendered more comprehensible by the choices made. Indeed, the choice to engage in increasingly symbolic politics did not reveal a reflexive movement ideology but an inchoate politic aimed at preserving radical, even utopian, postures. Left social movements of the time internalized elements of interest-group liberalism (pluralist-group identity) in contradictory ways (hence, the emphasis on the symbolic, the prefigurative, and the contradictory stance toward the state). These contradictory internalizations are best illustrated from the vantage point of the movements themselves; the movements' self-understandings of external constraints, while not always consistent, demonstrate an inability to thematize a link between symbolic stances and structural reform.

These self-understandings help explain the repertoires of ideology action available to NSMs today.

Three illustrative moments in the sixties demonstrate the impact of interest-group liberalism on the choices of social movements advocating social democracy and economic justice. In briefly isolating three frames (one from the SNCC, one from the Yippie! anti-war mobilization in Chicago, and one from Redstockings of the Women's Liberation Movement), I suggest that a convergence of factors can be identified in each of these instances that characterize the repertories available to NSMs in America. In each instance, the radical wing of the broader social movement (respectively, the Civil Rights movement, the anti-war movement, and the women's movement) was pushed further into symbolic action as a result of liberal elements being drawn into the orbit of interest-group politics. Concessions gained under these circumstances were limited and did nothing to favorably change the institutional arrangements for future movement challenges. The forces set against structural reform were significant and symbolic radicalism, while based on a desire to preserve an alternative path, was ultimately terribly isolating and ineffective in securing significant change.

STUDENT NON-VIOLENT COORDINATING COMMITTEE: THE RISE OF BLACK POWER

In his book, *Political Process and the Development of Black Insurgency*, author Doug McAdam suggests that the height of the Civil Rights movement occurred between 1961 and 1965. During those four years, formal movement organizations sponsored approximately 1,106 events. Between 1966 and 1970, the number had dropped to 819.[9] The four major Civil Rights organizations (NAACP, CORE, SNCC, and SCLC)[10] were credited with sponsoring 75 percent of all events for the 1961–1965 period, and just 56 percent in the 1966–1970 period. The general decline in Civil Rights events might suggest a lessened need for protest due to significant concessions. However, the diminished level of protest can be misleading: Many in the Civil Rights movement demonstrated an intense and significant ideological shift following many of those concessions. This shift did not suggest an amelioration of discontent, but rather a vexed and betrayed agenda. More than just a general decline, the Civil Rights movement was undergoing a dramatic ideological polarization that reflected the bifurcated trajectories discussed above.

Doug McAdam describes the polarization that marked the decline of the period 1966–1970 as existing between a nonviolent integrationist wing and a militant Black Power wing. He argues:

> Lined up on one side were traditional integrationists who continued to eschew violence as an unacceptable or ineffective means of pursuing movement goals. Aligned in increasing opposition to the integrationist was the so-called Black Power wing of the movement, with its rejection of integration as *the* fundamental goal of black insurgency and its approval of violence (either in self-defense or as an offensive tactic), as an acceptable addition to the movement's tactical arsenal.[11]

But in many respects, while the decline can be said in part to be the result of factional fighting within the Civil Rights movement, the labels ascribed here obscure the causes of the ideological polarization. The rise of black power within the Civil Rights movements had more to do with the *political* integration that resulted from interest-group co-optation of the 1961–1965 initiatives than with *racial* integration. And while the political co-optation was indeed interpreted by many black-power advocates in racial terms, its context was fundamentally political. The realization of the limits of electoral and institutional strategies in a climate of interest-group liberalism became painfully clear to many, particularly the black members of SNCC, in the wake of the Mississippi Freedom Democratic Party's (MFDP) rejection in Atlantic City in August 1963. That event demonstrated to many in the Civil Rights movements that the Democratic Party was willing to go only so far in accommodating the demands of black voters for equal access. It was a turning point for SNCC.

The voter registration efforts of an integrated SNCC in Mississippi during the summer of 1963 forged the basis for the MFDP. Under the banner of the MFDP, black Mississippians registered en masse for the first time and significantly challenged the Jim Crow obstacles to black registration. Those obstacles had systematically denied black Americans the franchise in Mississippi since Reconstruction. Threatening to break the fantastically racist stronghold of the white Citizen's Council on Mississippian politics, the SNCC and MFDP workers were harassed, beaten, and murdered that summer. Armed with proof that the all-white Democratic Party regulars planning to attend the national convention in Atlantic City that August did not represent the Democratic Party voters of Mississippi, and that in fact they had participated in, even orchestrated, campaigns of intimidation and unlawfulness in denying blacks the vote, the MFDP requested a hearing with the Credentials Committee of the Democratic Party to plead its case. It requested that the regular Mississippi delegation not be seated, and that the MFDP, as the lawful representatives of a nonracial Democratic Party, be given credentials instead. After a long and highly publicized battle within the party, the MFDP and the SNCC were pressured by moderate Civil Rights leaders and the Democratic Party to accept a compromise. Urging the MFDP to accept two token at-large votes alongside the all-white party regulars, it was also promised that the party would eliminate all racial discrimination in state party delegate-selection procedures before the next convention.

The pressure to accept deepened the schism in the Civil Rights movement. David Garrow, in *Bearing the Cross,* provides a glimpse into the dynamics of that decision:

> More administration pressure was exerted on movement leaders to persuade the MFDP to accept the Johnson offer. Roy Wilkins and Whitney Young recommended that the compromise be accepted. Rustin and Andrew Young advised King to speak out more strongly in favor of the proposal, and on Wednesday King joined other national movement figures at the MFDP's church headquarters to speak in favor of acceptance. Many in the MFDP delegation whispered that Rauh, Rustin, and King had sold them out.[12]

The division and sense of betrayal hit young SNCC activists particularly hard. While King and others sensed that such a compromise contributed a degree of victory to the movement, the cost, even in symbolic terms, was seen as much too high for those desiring more substantive concessions, for example, the party's immediate condemnation of segregationist state practices and acknowledging its history of supporting segregationist policies. Garrow argues that "the Atlantic City convention left the movement more shaken and divided than at any prior time." SNCC's long-held suspicion of the liberal elements of the Civil Rights movement seemed confirmed in the bitter disappointment caused by the Democratic Party's actions. In Atlantic City, many Civil Rights workers experienced, in the words of one participant, "the emptiness of traditional liberalism."[13]

Among those SNCC organizers most suspicious of the moderates in the Civil Rights movements was Stokely Carmichael. In 1965, Carmichael was elected chairman of SNCC. Between Atlantic City and his ascension to leadership, the organization began playing an increasingly uncompromising role in the Civil Rights movement. By 1966, under Carmichael's leadership, SNCC had popularized an intentionally ambiguous ideology of black power. The notion was indicative of a desire on the part of many younger participants to not rely on whites for help and to challenge what was considered a patronizing liberalism. Of course, it also generated an air of separation and intimidation in the minds of sympathetic liberals. At this time, SNCC leaders asked white SNCC participants to leave the organization and organize among whites instead. As a result, SNCC became a constant source of concern to those within the movement interested in legislative compromises and the Johnson administration's support.[14]

The notion of black power, however intentionally ambiguous, galvanized many who were discontent with the way the Civil Rights movement was proceeding. Black power was the first in a series of late-sixties identity claims deployed as a means of staking out a radical politics that could not, it was imagined, be co-opted by the institutions and ideology of liberalism in America. Ironically, the militancy and cultural exclusivity of the stance functioned to make the movement vulnerable to isolation. That isolation made the extreme governmental repression that was unleashed, particularly against the Black Panthers, even harder to deal with. Indeed, as Freedom of Information Act files suggest, the distrust and divisions that resulted from the separatist politics of the era were among the favorite fronts of attack for the FBI's "Cointelpro operation."[15]

The Democratic Party's redirection of the Civil Rights movement's most egalitarian and democratic potential produced a second stream of movement activity that rejected the seduction of interest-group liberalism, yet was equally constrained from realizing its goals. While the political betrayal of the Civil Rights movement's potential was premised on racism as well as an institutional bias against popular control, those unwilling to sell out relied on an identity-based politic that emphasized the racial bias but obscured the political and institutional supports of that bias. Ultimately, the cultural posture failed to offer an alternative strategy; while it provided a symbolic militancy, it was unable to translate the heightened rhetoric in a sustainable practice and strategy for reform.

Black power served an important function in many respects, and its emergence, given the institutional limits and ideological constraints of the era, has a logic. Its contribution to contemporary politics lies not so much in its direct lineage to current organizations, but as an illustrative memory of the unavoidable fork in the road: Movements willing to engage the

Democratic Party, even under the best conditions, as in the early movement when electoral leverage could be applied, are faced with the imminent deradicalizing of their agenda. And movements unwilling to accept the cost of institutional engagement must assume another form, another view. SNCC was evidence of the simultaneous necessity and difficulty of just such a move. Its cultural turn illustrates the limits of identity-based radicalism.

ABBIE HOFFMAN AND YIPPIE!: THEATER OF THE DISPLACED

The shadow of the MFDP outcome in Atlantic City in 1964 stretched all the way to Chicago in 1968, both in terms of Democratic Party machinations and movement repertoires. And while challengers in Chicago demonstrated against the party's support of the Vietnam war, the same liberal ideology and institutional limits that were present in Atlantic City were again present in Chicago. However, this time the challengers were informed by the experience of the MFDP and the militancy that swelled in the intervening years. The resultant decline of faith in institutional strategies and the rise of black power ideology in Civil Rights organizations like SNCC profoundly shaped the path of white anti-war movement activists. In the narrow frame of SNCC, whites who were asked to leave the organization in 1966 displayed a parallel ideological development—in lieu of institutional strategies, a focus on issues of identity, culture, and symbolic radicalism ensued.

Abbie Hoffman was one of those SNCC activists who was asked to leave the organization in 1966. For the two years he spent in Mississippi, beginning with the Freedom Summer project in 1964, Abbie Hoffman worked primarily on voter registration campaigns with SNCC. From his own account, he had a profoundly sobering experience with the MFDP at the Democratic National Convention in 1964. Reflecting on this, his first personal experience with the bankruptcy of formal institutional politics,[16] he would later title his book chapter on the convention "Being Right Is Not Enough." Hoffman's experience there, in light of his political influence in the anti-war movement, makes him an interesting example of the bifurcated worlds of symbolic radicalism and institutional strategies that defined the late sixties and early seventies.

For many of the young white activists in the Civil Rights movement, the largely liberal commitment to democratic rights and social justice that brought them into the movement underwent a dramatic transformation when confronted with the brutalities of Jim Crow and, what seemed to them, the intransigent and piecemeal efforts of the Democratic Party's leadership. Abbie Hoffman's political choices were limited in 1966 with the SNCC decision to become an all-black organization. SNCC's request for whites to organize in their "own communities" left many in need of a new base and a new set of concerns. For those who were no longer students, the choices were few. Abbie Hoffman, at thirty, was initially unsure of where to continue. He moved to the Lower East Side of New York City, where he chose to do "white support work" for the Civil Rights movement. There he opened up Liberty House, a cooperative that sold crafts made by southern black women in an effort to raise money for the movement down South. But in 1967, Stokely Carmichael advised Hoffman to turn the cooperative over to black management and encouraged him to organize against the Vietnam War.

Searching for new ways to protest the Vietnam War, Hoffman was struck by the sudden influx of young people into the East Side. Dubbed hippies by the press, Hoffman described them not as spoiled middle-class kids, but as poor rural teenagers—"uneducated and stoned, easy prey for sadists and pimps who set up crash pads as recruiting camps for prostitutes."[17] With other white organizers, Hoffman first began organizing the so-called hippies by providing social services through a New York City-funded community project. His initially cool reaction to apolitical hippies gradually shifted as he sensed a phenomenon that could potentially be transformed. Hoffman and friends made a conscious decision to attempt politicizing white youth by using the new cultural tendencies and technologies. Influenced by the writings of Francis Fanon and Antonin Artaud, they adopted a strategy of pranks to politicize the new cultural stream. In this sense, the cultural turn, already in place to some degree because of the SNCC terms, was embraced. Consciously adopting Situationist-inspired theater tactics carefully crafted for media consumption, "Yippie!" originators Bob Fass, Jim Fouratt, Hoffman, and others attempted to blend art, television, youth culture, and politics.

Yippie! was intentionally unbound by organizational accountability. Fashioned as a mechanism to bring the cultural movement and the political movements together, Yippie! was specifically launched with the Chicago Convention in mind. Yippie! organizers planned a "Festival of Life," featuring performers Phil Ochs, Allen Ginsberg, the Fugs, and Jefferson Airplane. From the idea's inception in January 1968, until the violent and widely publicized frenzy that occurred those August nights in Chicago, Yippie! efforts provoked strong reaction among embattled elements of the anti-war movement, including liberals in the Democratic Party and pacifists like Dave Dellinger of the Mobe, the largest anti-war organization in the country.

When initially conceived, the Yippie! plan was to protest the Johnson candidacy and challenge the "two parties of war." But the candidacies of Eugene McCarthy and Bobby Kennedy stalled agreement between any of the anti-war elements. Then Johnson's withdrawal, Kennedy's assassination, and Humphrey's assured nomination left the anti-war movement's strategy for Chicago in disarray. In the space created by ideological uncertainty and institutional lockout, the Yippie! plans gained disproportionate attention, in part because of their conscious efforts to use the media to project symbols aimed at mobilizing young people.

Yippie! referred to itself as a "myth." David Farber, in his book on the events in Chicago, recounts a piece written by Hoffman, who, as the date drew nearer, was concerned about the possible problems the myth was creating. Yippie! was generating response, but adequate facilities and plans were not secured due to city resistance. Farber relates:

> Hoffman began by explaining the Yippie!'s relationship to the myth. He wrote that Yippie! had four main objectives: the blending of pot and politics; the creation of a gigantic national get together; the development of a model for an alternative society; and the need to make some statement about LBJ, the Democratic Party, electoral politics, and the state of the nation. "To accomplish these tasks . . . requires the construction of a vast myth, for through the notion of a myth large numbers of people could get turned on and in the process of getting turned on, begin to participate in Yippie! and start to focus on Chicago. *Precision was sacrificed for a greater degree of suggestion . . .* and distortion became the life blood of Yippie!."[18] (original emphasis)

The Yippie! myth was seductive to the many young people who were being turned on to countercultural lifestyles but were politically inchoate. The use of famous rock bands as a drawing card (it should be noted that the advertised Jefferson Airplane never was confirmed and never did show) underscores this point.

Just as ideological differences in the Civil Rights movement reflected the bifurcated social movement choices available in an era of interest-group liberalism, a parallel existed in the anti-war movement. The explosion of youth culture (the baby boom, relative prosperity, FM rock, marijuana and LSD, sexual experimentation), which inspired the symbolic radicalism of Yippie!, was happening independently of both institutional politics and the politics of the "straight social" movements. In a situation where the war issue was proving to divide the Democratic Party, the efforts of the Mobe to affect the party's plank on the war seemed tenable. However, if, as Yippie! sensed, that institutional possibility would evaporate with the Humphrey nomination, the ingredients for a symbolic, cultural assault on the "system" appeared available and efficacious. While symbolic adventurism in the face of state repression may appear foolhardy, the choice made by the cultural radicals was not as inconceivable as, for example, Todd Gitlin has suggested in his books *The Whole World Is Watching* and *The Sixties*. While it is, in my view, an ideological turn that further obfuscates the real avenues of power to which social movements must in fact gain access, it is also true that "cultural assaults" like the one in Chicago were responsible for bringing tens of thousands of young people into the movement after 1968.[19] It is often noted that this influx occurred at the same time that movement (organizational) deterioration began. But, it is in keeping with my overall argument that regardless of the influx, the strain on and deterioration of social movement organizations was long under way before 1968 as a result of the lack of institutional options. It must be noted that no "radical" social movement at that time had the resources, strategy, or ideological coherence capable of translating that influx into a sustainable radical movement. But the causes of that political void are not located in the turn itself; it must be conceded, however, that the causes are not made more comprehensible by the move either. Stephen Bronner, in his balanced assessment in *Moments of Decision*, frames the available choices this way:

> Although it is difficult to believe today, the movement never gripped the majority of the American people until long after its demise. . . . And in this vein, the movement has often been criticized for its insularity. Perhaps there is an element of truth to the critique. But the question remains: what institutions and groups should have supported it? The Democratic Party was still, basically, more attached to the "guns and butter" thinking of Sen. Henry Jackson than to the progressive agenda advocated by Sen. George McGovern, while the Republicans opposed everything for which the movement stood. Even progressive churches, whatever their concern for civil rights and criticism of the Vietnam War, were often aghast at the movement's opposition to established mores and free sexuality. . . . Finally, as far as unionized workers were concerned, it is patently absurd to "blame" the New Left for not

achieving links with organizations that had been ideologically and politically corrupted at least since the anticommunist witch hunts following the Second World War.[20]

The politics of both the black power movement and the radical anti-war movement indicate the lure of symbolic, identity-based politics in an atmosphere where dominant ideological frameworks and institutional arrangements shut social movements out. Formal participation, limited to the deradicalizing, nonaccountable interest-group format, was an option only for those organizations and groups willing to accommodate both their rhetoric and demands to the parameters of American liberalism. The alternatives were increasingly defined in symbolic terms, by both the total rejection of the institutions and values of the dominant culture, and by the need to create, in Abbie Hoffman's terms, a model for an alternative society. An emphasis on the utopian moment, the prefigurative as Carl Boggs has indicated, was reflected in internal movement structures and processes. More than any other social movement, the women's movement of the late sixties and early seventies demonstrates not only the bifurcating effect of interest-group liberalism on social movement repertoires, but it also popularized those prefigurative processes and structures that are associated with NSMs today. One of the earliest and most influential of women's movement groups in this respect was Redstockings of the women's liberation movement.

REDSTOCKINGS: CONSCIOUSNESS-RAISING GONE AWRY

The participation of young women in radical social movements of the early 1960s paved the way for a convergence of women into what would later be dubbed the second wave of American feminism. The dissatisfaction of mostly white college-age women activists with both the male civil rights leadership and the white student movement leadership was in part responsible; the desire to forward an analysis of women's oppression within these respective movements was an overlapping and related impulse. The participation and dissatisfaction of women in both SNCC and Students for a Democratic Society (SDS) are illustrative examples of this trend.

During these years, women on the Left were experiencing a growing sense of frustration and alienation from the movement to which they had dedicated so much time and energy with little recognition. For the young women working in the South (both black and white), the experience of working with skilled black female leaders like Ella Baker and Fanny Lou Hamer did much to raise their expectations of themselves and of the young men who dominated the leadership and often ignored their talents. For those in SDS who challenged male leadership openly, the experience was rife with humiliating castigations for not being truly "revolutionary."

By 1967, SDS was riddled with factionalism and uncertain of its future; by the same year, whites in SNCC had been asked to leave the organization and organize in their own communities. These factors led to an energized convergence of women in New York City that year. What followed was the founding of one of the original organizations of the women's liberation movement: New York Radical Women. In an interview with Rosalyn Baxandall, a founding member, she describes the convergence:

> It was really a combination of things. I can tell you a lot of women came from SNCC: Elizabeth Sutherland, Carol Hanisch, Kathie Sarachild, and Sandra Casey. Others from different places. I mean this is 1967 and the call from SNCC was "whites go into your own community and organize on your own issues." As a result, many women ended up in New York to form this group for women's liberation. By 1968, all these women came together to form New York Radical Women: Kathie Sarachild, Ellen Willis, Robin Morgan, Shuli Firestone, Ann Koedt, Kate Millet, myself, and on and on. It was a great group and it just kept growing.[21]

Drawing on their experiences in both the Civil Rights movement and the student movement, these women brought with them an emphasis on participatory democracy (an early SDS notion) and the tactics of symbolic protest (the sit-in and pickets used in SNCC.) For their own purposes, consciousness-raising (CR) emerged as a centerpiece for New York Radical Women. The basic premise of feminist CR was that the study of women's lives, their own lives, would suggest an action agenda. They were influenced by two distinct sources. The first was the use of CR-type formations by women in the Chinese Revolution (recall the high regard the Chinese Revolution was enjoying among many U.S. radicals at this time). The second was the experience with CR-like training in the Civil Rights movement to prepare young whites for the bus rides down South during Freedom Summer.

In the first case, William Hinton's book on the Chinese Revolution, *Fanshen,* depicted a village in which the women held meetings to talk about the problems in their lives as women and about overcoming them in political ways.[22] The Chinese slogan used to describe this process was "speaking bitterness to recall bitterness," and that became a popular phrase in New York Radical Women. In the second case, in preparation for the dangerous rides down South, nonviolence training employed by CORE and SNCC had participants sit in a circle and talk about their fears and how they would react to threatening situations. The goals in this context were to aid in the development of group identity, to promote unity, and to help overcome hardship.

An early example of the use of the technique within New York Radical Women can be seen in the discussions that led to the Miss America protest during the summer of 1968. Carol Hanisch, in a November 1968 article, recalls:

> The idea came out of our group method of analyzing women's oppression by recalling our own experiences. We were watching "Schmearguntz," a feminist movie, one night at our meeting. The movie had flashes of the Miss America contest in it. I found myself sitting there remembering how I had felt at home with my family watching the pageant as a child, an adolescent, and a college student. I knew it had evoked powerful feelings. When I proposed the idea to our group, we decided to go around the room with each woman telling how she felt about the pageant. We discovered that many who put the pageant down, still watched it. Others like myself, had consciously identified with it, and cried with the winner. From our communal thinking came the concrete plans for action. We all agreed that our main point in the demonstration would be that all women were hurt by beauty competition— Miss America as well as ourselves.[23]

As a measure of their newfound theory of social change, the Miss America Protest brought enormous success, but in the same way that symbolic action at Chicago brought success. The event gave organizers a sense that they were having an impact on the culture, but it also testified to the limits of the political context within which they were enmeshed. Their own organizational styles and self-understandings did little to secure the kinds of economic and political gains needed for sustained impact. The Miss America Protest brought the ideas of feminism into America's living rooms, but it also placed more weight on the group than their organization, built on open meetings and little structure, could tolerate. In addition, the lack of ideological coherence and goals became painfully obvious as the influx began. Rosalyn Baxandall recounts:

> We got so much coverage from the thing . . . I mean afterwards too. There were a lot of national TV appearances. I was on the David Susskind show I remember, and several others. But it was almost too much coverage. It was more exposure than we were prepared to deal with, organizationally. There were so many letters, hundreds of letters from all over the country supporting the protest. We just couldn't answer them all. We couldn't even open some of them. We threw hundreds out.[24]

Not only was the mail unmanageable, ideological differences began to emerge, reflecting the increasing internalization of limited political leverage. Disagreements as to the purpose and uses of CR caused splits among members. Many in the group saw CR as a therapeutic, small-group process that should not be tied to direct action. To those within New York Radical Women who were dedicated to the actionist intention of CR, this represented a growing trend away from political action. The action-oriented women split off and formed Redstockings, who, as the class-conscious wing of the movement, were responsible for popularizing "the personal is political" and for launching critiques of both the apolitical trend toward cultural feminism and the interest-group policies of liberal feminists. Ultimately, however, Redstockings was unable to sustain its agenda amid the two trends. Problems in focus, forms, and strategies plagued their work.

The influential phrase "the personal is political" was initially conceived as linking women's experience of oppression and exploitation to objective conditions that could be identified through the process of CR. The phrase held a distinct meaning for Redstockings members:

> We wanted to talk about and organize around things that had to do with women's lives: abortion, day care, sex. These things were thought to be personal and we were showing that they were very political . . . you might think it's personal to get raped, but when you talk to others it becomes political. That was the power of the whole thing. That we could translate what had been regarded as personal into political acts.[25]

Less political interpretations of the phrase prevailed among many in the broader movement. Cultural and lifestyle-oriented approaches to feminism began to usurp the meaning of the phrase.[26] The small group, initially a direct action-inspired arrangement, was transformed into a place where personal identity was explored in relation to broader political themes. "The personal is political" was evolving into a nonaction-oriented phrase that equated personal transformation with political transformation. Institutional connections were being lost.

Between 1968 and 1970, Redstockings engaged in a variety of actions including disrupting New York State abortion hearings, picketing the sex-segregated classified ads in the *New York Times*, campaigning for public day care, and crashing a bridal fair in New York City, where they released white mice into the crowd. By 1970, though, political actions by women's organizations had declined significantly. Redstockings members saw the decline as a result of co-optation of feminism by liberal feminists willing to engage in interest-group politics. In several essays, the critique of the liberal feminist "takeover" is without reserve:

> Today the women's liberation movement is in the hands of liberal oppor-tunists, and therefore in the hands of the Left/liberal male establishment. These women—*Ms.* magazine, some of the *Village Voice* writers, and the "women's lib ladies" in communities all over the country—are scrambling after the few crumbs that men have thrown out when we radicals began to expose the truth and demand some changes. These are the women who have access to press and money. They are supposedly "the leaders" of the women's movement, but they are leading us down the road to a few re-spectable reforms and nothing more.[27]

The co-optation of the women's liberation movement by liberal forces was only compounded by the continuous struggle among more radical el-ements over notions of organization and leadership. The emphasis on the prefigurative, the process of CR, and the rotation of spokespersons were among the issues that made it difficult to sustain continuity within the or-ganization. For many in Redstockings, the inability of the women's liber-ation movement to develop some form of coordinated federation, along-side the failure to implement notions of democratic accountability, made sustained activity impossible. Many women simply burned out. Jo Free-man's discussion of the problems of organizational style within these seg-ments of the women's movement is made clear in her essay, "The Tyranny of Structurelessness," written under the pseudonym Joreen. Here she identifies the problems of accountability and leadership in small groups that eschew hierarchy and formal organization.[28]

Like the Black Power movement and the theatrical politics of Yippie!, the radical women's movement failed to sustain itself. Its contributions, while memorable, were not made concrete. While it can be argued that the radicalism evident in all these groups exerted pressure on more liberal elements, in concrete terms radicalism in this era becomes divorced from its own set of institutional demands or vision. The radical women's movement is no different in this regard.

In all three instances (SNCC, Yippie!, and Redstockings), the emphasis on issues of identity, symbolic action, and organizational fluidity reflects the limited repertoires available to democratic social movements in the United States that stand in opposition to liberalism. Historically, the ability of social movements to have an impact was dependent on a climate of electoral instability. Even then, protest movements exploiting an unstable electoral climate were drawn into major-party politics and/or reconstituted by interest-group liberalism. Such a reconstitution has most often meant the dropping of substantive economic demands—a reminder of the sound ideological defeat of class politics in America. Once drawn in structurally, and then ideologically, social movements have proven incapable of gaining support for institutional reform (e.g., campaign finance reform) that might support social movement influence and increased accountability.

At the same time, movements of the sixties that retained a radical posture were prone to an internal focus on prefigurative organizational forms and an external focus that became increasingly symbolic and uninterested in accessing existing institutions. These two traits were bridged by an ideological emphasis on identity—black power, youth culture, women's experience. Social movements today are still vulnerable to the bifurcating tendencies of interest-group pluralism. Indeed, the situation has in many respects only grown worse due to a less competitive electoral climate and a more conservative atmosphere. Even those movement sectors that, in their liberal incarnation, made it into the orbit of interest-group politics, have, since the eighties, found themselves dethroned and marginalized. Unfortunately, sixties' innovations in social movement repertoires persist (though no serious cross-generational institutions persist). The available ideological repertoires have ultimately done little to overcome the dilemma of bifurcation.

NOTES

1. See George Katsiafikas, *The Imagination of the New Left: A Global Analysis of 1968* (Boston: South End Press, 1987).

2. See Stephen Eric Bronner, *Moments of Decision* (New York: Routledge Press, 1989). Here Bronner focuses on turning points in the history of political radicalism of the twentieth century in an effort to "clarify the structure in which contingent events took place as well as their *political* significance" (p. 3).

3. Claus Offe, "NSMs: Challenging the Boundaries of Institutional Politics," *Social Research*, vol. 52, n. 4 (Winter 1985), p. 829.

4. See Claus Offe, *Contradictions of the Welfare State*, John Keane, ed. (London: Hutchinson, 1984).

5. The unequal bargaining of interest groups that privilege elite and business interests in the policy-making process has been documented in the work of Tierney and Schlozman in *Organized Interest and American Democracy* (New York: Harper and Row, 1986).

6. Theodore Lowi, *The End of Liberalism*, p. 62.

7. Of course, in the past fifteen years, there have been attempts on the part of electorally minded social movement coalitions to overcome this pattern of bifurcation. The history and denouement of the Rainbow Coalition (at first building on the radical Civil Rights tradition), however, confirm my unhappy prognosis as to the viability of the current electoral system. Some encouraging efforts have been mounted by the New Party, Green USA, and other parties that combine significantly radical elements of labor with a social movement base. In these efforts, the electoral context itself has become a target for reform. Unfortunately, resistance is significant and the efforts too disparate for a more serious incursion to have been made.

8. Various accounts of the struggle by the Mississippi Freedom Democratic Party in Atlantic City at the 1964 Democratic National Convention support this claim. In particular, see David Garrow, *Bearing the Cross: Martin Luther King, Jr., and the Southern Christian Leadership Conference* (New York: Vintage Books, 1986); Doug McAdams, *Political Process and the Development of Black Insurgency* (Chicago: University of Chicago Press, 1982); and the PBS documentary "Eyes on the Prize: Mississippi . . ."

9. Doug McAdam, *Political Process and the Development of Black Insurgency*, Table 8.1, p.183.

10. National Association for the Advancement of Colored People; Congress on Racial Equality; Student Non-Violent Coordinating Committee; and the Southern Christian Leadership Conference.

11. Doug McAdam, *Political Process and the Development of Black Insurgency*, p.184.

12. David Garrow, *Bearing the Cross*, p. 350.

13. Ibid., p. 351.

14. Carmichael's own writings, "What We Want" and "Toward a Black Liberation," detail his own understanding of black power. Also see *Newsweek,* August 22, 1966, pp. 33–35, and *Dissent,* February 1967, pp. 69–79.

15. See Brian Glick's *Cointelpro* (Boston: South End Press, 1989).

16. See Abbie Hoffman's *Soon to Be a Major Motion Picture* (New York: Putnam, 1980) for a detailed account of his work in electoral politics prior to *Mississippi Summer*.

17. Ibid., p. 82.

18. David Farber, *Chicago '68* (Chicago: University of Chicago Press, 1988), pp. 45–46.

19. See Kirkpatrick Sale's *SDS* for details. On page 479 he reports that at least dozens of new chapters were started the first few weeks of the school term after Chicago, and that more than 100 new chapters formed by the end of the semester, raising SDS chapters to 350. In addition, note the use of language used by SDS members Bill Ayers and Terry Robbins in the leaflet following Chicago. Clearly, the counter-cultural style was a drawing card for SDS.

20. Stephen Bronner, *Moments of Decision* (New York: Routledge, 1992), p. 108.

21. Interview with Rosalyn Baxandall, New York, March 1989 (unpublished).

22. See also Elizabeth Croll's *Feminism and Socialism in China* (New York: Schocken Books, 1980).

23. Carol Hanisch, "What Can Be Learned: A Critique of the Miss America Pageant" in *Voices from Women's Liberation*, edited by Leslie Tanner (New York: New American Library, 1970), p. 133.

24. Interview with Rosalyn Baxandall.

25. Ibid.

26. For an extended discussion of factions within the radical women's movement, see Alice Echols, *Daring to Be Bad* (Minneapolis: University of Minnesota Press, 1989).

27. Carol Hanisch, "The Liberal Take-Over of the Women's Liberation Movement," in *Feminist Revolution* (New York: Random House, 1975), p. 163.

28. Joreen (also known as Jo Freeman), "The Tyranny of Structurelessness," in *Feminist Revolution* (New York: Random House, 1975), p. 163.

Chapter Five

Dis-Unity and New Social Movements: A Look at the 1980s Student Movement in the United States

For some it comes as news that throughout the 1980s, there was a grass-roots revival of student politics in the United States, most markedly since approximately 1985. In 1990, a University of California (Berkeley) policy institute conducted a national survey from which they concluded that over 30 percent of first-year college students had already participated in a demonstration around a social or political cause, including the environment, abortion rights, and community anti-drug events. While some older (1960s) activists, forgetting their more meager beginnings, were minimally impressed with such an indicator, eighties participants saw the study as conformation of an established student movement. Unlike the early sixties, however, student activists of the eighties faced a far tougher economic climate and frequently suffered from a misconception about their numbers when compared with the previous era of protest.

Through various media portrayals of the sixties, young people engaging in social protest in the eighties and early nineties often perceived themselves to be numerically far behind. This is not to suggest that they longed for the sixties, but many, nonetheless, operated under the impression that "back then" everybody was involved. Undeniably, student movement activity between 1985 and 1992 reached substantial levels, yet the movement itself was consigned to relative obscurity.

Caricatures of the typical 1980s student present an image of greed and political apathy. The gap between reality and stereotype can, in part, be explained by the inability of the 1980s student movement to project itself nationally. This inability can be related to the inherited catalogue of social movement ideologies and practices, which proved to be less than useful in the 1980s climate. Many inheritances from the 1960s proved troublesome to 1980s students who were operating under a more restricted economic and cultural climate. Ironically, those elements of social movement history transmitted to young people in the 1980s are precisely the developments that helped preserve an oppositional stance for the previous generation. A parallel pattern of bifurcation can be identified within the student movement in the 1980s. For those groups who rejected the limits of interest-group organization and politics, the available repertoires with regard to forms, ideological aims, and political focus proved to be both confusing and dissipating.

The great upheavals of the 1960s and early 1970s were largely driven by young people and yet were the result of the efforts of a dedicated small minority of the general population. The Civil Rights movement, the anti-Vietnam War movement, the women's movement, the Black Power movement, the Poor People's movement, and the counterculture generally, all possessed large numbers of students and youth in their base. It has been suggested that, in large part, the demography of the 1960s American population accounts for this energetic upsurge by youth. However, additional factors, like the growth of the middle class and the expansion of social welfare programs (which were responsible for the unprecedented numbers of first-generation university admits, including the numbers of working-class youth) have also been suggested as explanation.

Certainly, a large youth population, relative prosperity, technological developments in media, and higher education levels are all factors. The sheer spectacle of the era aided the 1960s movements with a degree of success. The student movement of the 1980s, while possessed of technological abilities and similar educational levels, did not have a comparable demographic base, either numerically or economically. The lower birth rates of the 1960s and early 1970s, combined with a contracted economic climate in the 1980s, would suggest a less daring and smaller movement, if one at all. But the student movement of the 1980s and early 1990s engaged tens of thousands of students across the country. The ratio of participants to overall population at various points equaled the 1960s ratios. So why then has the student movement of the 1980s remained a kind of secret?

In large part, the student movement of the 1980s has gone unrecognized due to its inability to discern and engage, either ideologically or strategically, the institutional and economic context in which it is enmeshed. This inability is a legacy embedded within the patterns of movement ideology and action passed on from the sixties. The ideological developments of the sixties represented a break with old Left frameworks which, while initially powerful in their symbolic function, have not, over time, provided an adequate basis for sustained political power struggles. In effect, student movements today, operating within the NSM paradigm spawned by the movements of the sixties, have run into severe organizational and ideological obstacles that inhibit them from making an impact despite their relative strength in numbers.

More than just a question of strategy and tactics, the movements of the 1960s presented future generations with symbolic approaches lacking in reflexive practices. Symbolic stances may indeed be purposeful, given institutional limits, as was and too often is, the case. However, the "cultural turn" often denied participants a basis from which to consider their position in relation to the institutional, ideological, and economic context. As a result, the emphasis on autonomy, identity, community, and decentralization became reified in movement ideology and failed to comprehend the conditions that inspired the tack. Separated from reflexive strategy with respect to institutions, radical social movements today generally fail to present viable alternatives. As such, they exist as little more than an umbra of interest-group liberalism.

The first focus of this section will be to summarize the waves of U.S. student (and youth) movement formations dating from approximately 1985 to 1991, and to explore the correspondence between these formations and select NSM theories (Offe, Touraine, Melucci, and Laclau and Mouffe.) Throughout, I will argue, on two points in particular, that NSM theory offers inadequate support for its claims that the causes of these movement adaptations are definitively structural in nature—a result of global, economic, or bureaucratic shifts—and that these adaptations are contestational. Second, I will focus on specific features of NSMs that have proved problematic for sustained political action within the 1980s student movement (a contradictory stance toward the state, an emphasis on the prefigurative, and a nonreflexive identity politics). To demonstrate these problems, I will analyze the processes and results of two promising moments for political consensus and contestation: the national student anti-apartheid organizing of 1985 and the anti-Gulf War student and youth coalition of 1991. I will argue that the practical political consequences of NSM practice among U.S. students has resulted in ideological confusion and political (as well as organizational) collapse. The ideological posture and attendant organizational forms of NSM practice, I will argue, seriously retard sustained activity, democratic decision making, and organizational accountability. As a result, the student movement of the 1980s and 1990s relied on an overestimated symbolic radicalism that was unable to substantively challenge economic or political centers of power and either fell prey to the seduction of interest-group liberalism or simply collapsed. These trends, I argue, reflect a "postmodern" moment for NSMs that echoes the symbolic democracy of pluralist politics in America. Ultimately, NSM theory, whether of the New Modernity or Postmodern variety, is starkly insufficient as an explanation of, or catalyst for, real political power struggles.

THE NEW STUDENT MOVEMENT: 1985 TO 1991

At no point since the end of the Vietnam War has there been a total absence of student activism on U.S. campuses. The idea that there was a moment when "the sixties" died is misleading and false. At the same time, it is true that there have been rather poignant periods of retrenchment. More than focusing on the causes of retrenchment in the seventies and early eighties, I would rather quickly paint, with broad brush strokes, the bridge of issues and movement institutions that sustained the historical memory and practices of movement politics and brought us to the student movement in 1985.

When the Vietnam War ended, the issues that punctuated the political landscape of U.S. campuses and high schools included institutional sexism, ecological defense, lesbian and gay rights, minority faculty and student retention, ethnic and gender studies programs, Affirmative Action campaigns in the wake of the Bakke decision, opposition to draft registration after President Carter's reinstatement of it, and anti-nuclear energy and weaponry campaigns.

Organizational forms did not differ in large degree from the loose-knit campus affiliates of the 1960s except that there were no national multi-issue networks or organizations like SNCC or SDS in existence. The symbolic radicalism of the late sixties gave way to heightened isolation, ideological rigidity, and extreme militancy by the early seventies. The ideological splits and division of the mid-1970s gave way to what G. Oloffson has called "groupiscules." Oloffson makes the interesting observation that, in Germany, the 1970s witnessed the development of a variety of minuscule left-wing orthodox parties that, after collapse, spread out into a variety of small groups with high levels of ideological unity. In an effort to develop a broader base and recapture some of the previous popularity, the small groups consciously adopted NSM forms and lowered the level of ideological demands. The case can easily be made for the United States, as well, where NSM formations like the Midwest-based Progressive Student Network, founded in 1980, can be traced to ideological splits relating back to the Revolutionary Youth Movement 2 (RYM2), a seventies faction of SDS. However, these groupiscules are not the only social movement "institutions" of ideological transmission. Significant ideological transmission can be linked to the survival of black student unions throughout the seventies and into the eighties. Additionally, the founding of institutions like Movemiento de Estudiantes Chicano de Atzlan (MECHA) in 1968, and the reconstitution of the United States Student Association (USSA) in 1974 (after its predecessor, the National Student Association, experienced government infiltration), while not "Left" in constitution, did provide continuity, space, and resources during periods of retrenchment. Both MECHA and USSA, despite their interest-group character, acted as bridges for student organizing and embodied the conflict between the two paths of social movement development.

The various radical U.S. traditions operated and intermingled within 1980s and 1990s student movement at a rather unconscious level. A consequence of the sixties legacy was that few movement institutions were sustained where young people could actually train and study. Lacking reflexive spaces and traditions, the passing on of social movement history occurred irregularly. Eighties activists tended, as a result, to lack adequate historical knowledge of even the most recent era of political protest. Often unaware of this limitation, many student activists of the 1980s and 1990s experienced their work in distorted contexts and felt frustrated and isolated. Their sense of isolation was not imaginary. The relative obscurity of 1980s and 1990s student movement was conditioned and compounded by the lack of contact with the previous generation—as either allies or mentors. The "break with the old" so characteristic of the New Left, while liberating in many respects, did not suit the needs of the 1980s and 1990s activists. Yet the pattern continues by default. The failure of the 1960s movements to establish lasting institutions of change or cultural and historical memory proved to be a negative consequence of NSM fluidity.

One exception to this observation would be the southern Civil Rights community where mentoring is still a strong tradition. Community organizations and black churches, as political space, still play a role, and young activists coming out of this tradition tend to exhibit a higher ideological understanding of what they are doing and where they want to go. Aside from this set of institutions, the next two most common means of political education of 1980s and 1990s student activists tended to be either individual professors who had some connection to the sixties and seventies, and the groupiscules of various ideological persuasions that have demonstrated uncanny staying power. In combination, social movement repertoires trickled down through these means.

Interestingly, the sixties and seventies have, by a variety of these measures, left regional marks on current student organizing styles. In the 1980s and 1990s, student movement collectives, with tactics more akin to the anarchist or situationist traditions, predominated in some California schools, in New England-area schools, and in some parts of the Midwest. Within these, consensus decision making was preferred, and leadership was eschewed. While some Northeast urban and southern campus activists evidenced a stronger tendency toward organization building and traditional representative structures, the dominant trend was toward fluid, local organization. In both cases, competing tendencies existed.

In terms of issues, the early eighties witnessed the continuation and organizational expansion of grass roots student campaigns whose shifting articulations were influenced by the changing tide of domestic and foreign policies under the newly elected Reagan regime. Student politics reflected a wide range of issues with counterparts in nonstudent social movements: Central American solidarity work around the Sandinista Revolution, El Salvador, and Guatemala; two strands of women's rights work, on the one hand the campaign for the Equal Rights Amendment and, on the other, the campaigns by Women Against Pornography and other cultural feminists; and the No Nukes movement, which was one of the few issues that spawned a national student formation at this time—United Campuses to Prevent Nuclear War.

By 1983, however, the majority of U.S. campuses experienced a lull in student activism. Established student organizations like the United States Student Association, the very young Democratic Socialists of America–Youth Section (DSA–YS), and the Progressive Student Network (PSN) were among those struggling to grasp the staggering impact of Reaganomics on the lives of young people inside, outside, and teetering on the edge of the university orbit.

With broadly defined areas of engagement, student-oriented formations such as USSA, PSN, and DSA–YS frequently operated under a hit-or-miss strategy while looking for a galvanizing issue among students. Single-issue, non-student-defined organizations like the Committee in Solidarity with the People of El Salvador, founded in 1980, got off to a slow start on U.S. campuses. The climate among those who shared a general social justice agenda was seemingly one of strategic disorientation until the international anti-Apartheid campaigns in 1984 and 1985, headed by the African National Congress (ANC), revamped their long-standing appeals to campus-based anti-racism, social justice organizations in the United States.

The history of anti-racism campus groups in the United States working on the anti-apartheid issue dates back to 1966, yet the issue of university divestment was now a well-defined plank in a highly visible international campaign. The 1985 campus divestment movement occurred within the context and momentum of an international anti-apartheid strategy (headed by the ANC), which included United Nations backing and increased media coverage. The ANC provided a wavering and localized U.S. student movement with a political issue packing great moral imperative, an international context of debate, and a ready-made strategy aimed at university divestment from companies doing business in South Africa.

Consensus among student and youth organizers at this time is unanimous that the anti-apartheid campaigns of 1985 gave shape, recognition (both among students and the country), and identity to an otherwise amorphous and vaguely connected post-seventies generation of young activists. (Below I will discuss in more detail the anatomy of this movement both organizationally and ideologically.) The significance here is that it was the first broadly shared national organizing experience for this generation of young people. It provided a glimpse into the real strength and diversity a coordinated student movement might possess; it also provided a glimpse into the legacy of the late-sixties movements riddled with factionalism, racialism, sexism, and overly symbolic radicalism. Additionally, this juncture in U.S. student movement history first marked the persistent debates among students over the effectiveness and legitimacy of discrete local and regional formations with their concomitant attachment to direct democracy.

The 1985 anti-apartheid campaign that swept U.S. college campuses engaged hundreds of thousands of young people. Its successful tactics directly forced more than 130 U.S. colleges and universities to at least partially divest holdings from companies doing business in apartheid South Africa. As one component of an internationally coordinated effort, the U.S. student movement can claim a modest share of pride in the release of and eventual election of Nelson Mandela and the democratic transformation of South Africa. Its impact on the U.S. student movement also was profound. After 1985, an apparent explosion of grass roots campus organizations revived social movement discourse and activism in a manner not apparent among young people since the 1960s. A gamut of social and political issues captured the attention of tens of thousands of young people on U.S. campuses. The anti-apartheid movement of the mid-eighties was a watershed event that inspired political consciousness among American youth and opened the floodgate of unresolved ideological and practical conflicts raised by the 1960s movements.

Beginning in 1986, a well-articulated, though loosely connected series of anti-CIA campus protests emerged. Their demands generally reflected the strategy used in the anti-apartheid campaigns: How can an institution of higher learning, founded on democratic, humanist principles, provide institutional support for anti-democratic forces and human rights violators? Students protested the CIA's right to recruit on campuses with university support and assistance. They raised both international issues (as was the case in the South Africa protests) and those concerning undemocratic governing practices within the university, for example, the students' right to have a voice in the policies and practices of the university community. The anti-CIA campaigns were given a boost when Amy Carter, the former president's daughter—along with then-campus lecturer and student adviser, Abbie Hoffman—were arrested with seventy-two other students in November 1986 on the University of Massachusetts campus in Amherst. The ensuing Northampton, Massachusetts jury trial, largely crafted by Hoffman (legally representing himself) and primarily argued by Len Weinglass, upheld the students' right to commit civil disobedience against the CIA on the grounds of the Necessity Defense—that is, a small crime may be excused if it is committed while attempting to prevent the commission of a more significant crime. Key witnesses for the defense included international law experts, ex-CIA agents, and witnesses of Contra-war atrocities including medical volunteers in the war zones. The all-white, largely middle-class jury quickly found for the students.

The anti-CIA campaigns, sparked in 1986, spawned an extended agenda of anti-militarism as it related to university complicity: Students protested the Reserve Officer Training Corps; faculty contracts with the Pentagon, the CIA, and the NSA; and any identifiable university underwriting of military-related research. These campaigns were sporadically extended into targeted high schools where military recruitment was particularly heavy. In this case, campus activists bid for equal time to present alternatives to the military.

Around 1987, organizations such as USSA, DSA-YS, and PSN appeared to be under-representing this new wave of student protest. The experience of developing campaigns on the local level, while being inspired by often sketchy reports from other campuses (coupled with the recent memory of national waves of anti-apartheid protests of 1985) sparked in some the desire to build stronger links with fellow campus activists. In early 1986 the National Public Interest Research Group (Ralph Nader) funded two student activists to set up an office in Washington, D.C., under the name National Student Action Center (NSAC). There it published the most widely circulating newsletter reporting on campus activism of the 1980s. Abbie Hoffman, eager to find an entity into which he could channel addresses and names (which he picked up while on his national campus lecture circuit) worked with NSAC to help expand its mailing list. He also encouraged it to expand its newsletter service into a coordinated national organizational structure. It was Hoffman's sense from his experience lecturing on college campuses nationally that a new sensibility was underfoot and that it would require a more stable organizational form. In his letters at this time, he urges activists to concentrate on organizing skills and to build national democratic structures, "the likes of SNCC and early SDS."[1] It is worth noting that in Hoffman's talks to 1980s student activists nationally, he never suggested a return to Yippie-style politics.

At around this time, Hoffman worked with Rutgers University students who took up his challenge to hold National Student Convention '88 (he suggested the name). Hoffman astutely sensed students' desires for greater coordination. At NSC '88, students invited from around the country would discuss the prospect of founding a "mass-based, democratically structured organization with accountable leadership."[2] The Rutgers students were typical of this aforementioned unabsorbed wave of activism, and they sincerely desired to build something lasting. They were multi-issue in orientation and, as it soon became obvious, unacquainted with national organizing taboos and the entrenched attachment to localism. It was a moment in which it became evident that because those groups engaged in national student organizing were largely styled as interest groups (USSA, NSAC), national efforts became equated with co-optation and localism was perceived as radical. In April 1987, the Rutgers students issued a rather provocative open call for a February 1988 meeting. Tony Valella characterizes the seven hundred students who showed up:

> Students generally represented three different positions: (1) affiliated with existing national organizations, either student groups or sectarian political groups with their own views on the idea of a new national organization starting up; (2) dedicatedly not affiliated, independent, focused on local and regional actions, and unwilling to be categorized by labels and ideologies of the past; (3) those in the middle—the largest number by far—who were not yet affiliated, but who believed in the need to act politically, and who came to deliberate, investigate, question, and possibly leave with a new vehicle to execute their beliefs. As the weekend wore on, the positions of the two smaller groups overtook the less focused intentions of the students in the middle.[3]

No new organization was formed that weekend, but there was wide agreement that the event provoked a great deal of previously suppressed debate and raised the issues of organization, accountability, and consolidation to new levels. Even activists like Ray Davis of D.C. Student Coalition against Apartheid and Racism, who criticized the call as premature, later referred to it as a "watershed event."

By spring of 1988, campus campaigns remained loosely connected but even more widespread. Significant trends of activism were established along a host of interconnecting issues. Students mobilized to reverse the erosion of ethnic and gender studies programs and to demand university response to increased racist attacks on campus; unacknowledged sexual violence and harassment; and the blatant rise in homophobic attacks and harassment. By 1989, a clear educational rights agenda began to emerge as rising tuition costs exacerbated the paltry student federal assistance pot. The concern over prohibitive tuition costs was framed in such a way that campaigns frequently raised the principle of access in relation to discriminatory practices affecting African American, Latino, Asian, and other young minority populations. The main proponents of this analysis were groups led by students of color or students based at public universities with a diverse student body (e.g., the City University of New York [CUNY]). It was also in the spring of 1989 that the successful Howard University student takeover protesting Republican Lee Atwater's appointment to the Board of Trustees made national headlines.

Additionally, 1989 witnessed a renewed women's rights agenda focusing on reproductive rights, as well as crossover organizing campaigns between "pro-choice" groups, campus chapters of ACT-UP, and lesbian and gay associations on the issue of AIDS. Amid these waves of activism, there remained limited coordination between campuses outside of information sharing, or what is generally termed "networking."

Unable to develop any national agenda, National Student Convention '88 had ended with the call to develop regional networks; several were started, such as the New England Student Action Network, but proved short-lived. Between 1988 and 1989, several national student organizations were founded, making significant dents in the anti-national trend evidenced at Rutgers in early 1988. Among those organizations founded during this period were the Student Environmental Awareness Coalition (SEAC), the National Black Collegiate Caucus, Student Action Union (university democracy), Students Organizing Students (reproductive rights), and the Youth Greens-USA. Without a doubt, several mass mobilizations and events organized by or substantially composed of students provided inspiration and strength to these national attempts.

Four defining events among students stand out: the May 1989 CUNY student strike in which the CUNY system was effectively shut down; the April 1989 NOW-sponsored pro-choice march in Washington, D.C., in which young people (mostly women) comprised, even by NOW estimates, a plurality of the ranks; the October 1990 SEAC "Catalyst" conference, for which 7,000 young people traveled to Champaign, Illinois, to network on environmental issues; and the numerically smaller, yet defining African-American Students March on Washington in June 1990. This last event demonstrated the desire for national articulation despite the rhetorical adherence to local organizing. This event, like many efforts in 1989, expressed a building momentum of action that was outstripping the ideological attachments to decentralization and fragmentation. Activist-author Ray Davis has observed that the event was a culmination of energy "built upon other African-American and students of color organizing in the late 1980s such as the work of the People of Color Coalition/Stanford, the United Coalition Against Racism/Michigan, and the nationally significant takeover at Howard University in the spring of 1989 among others."[4]

The next two years of student activism indicated a continuation of many of the same issues but evidenced a greater degree of networking, national meetings and conferences, intraorganizational endorsements of specific campaigns, and a general curiosity on the part of student activists concerning the depth, breadth, and diversity of student activism around the country. Several national clearinghouses were set up around specific campaigns such as the CIA OFF-CAMPUS clearinghouse, funded by the Chicago Bill of Rights Foundation. And yet, despite these moves toward more coordinated action, the new student movement lacked any real consensus on the general goals, organizational requirements, or political basis for sustained coordination.

Contradictions surface in the push and pull of a movement that is growing, yet is unprepared strategically or ideologically for that growth. In this sense, the new student movement embodied many of the descriptions offered by NSM theorists, yet it also provides a basis for critique. Whereas NSM theory suggests that decentralization, an emphasis on autonomy from the state, and identity-based claims are structural responses that are contestational, they do not, I suggest, provide adherents with effective means of political engagement. Indeed, NSM practices as described by theorists de-emphasize the political character of such developments and, as such, diminish the degree of agency available to social movement participants.

Participants, specifically U.S. participants, adhere to available repertoires, in large part, without reflexive contemplation of either the conditions that shaped those patterns or how their current conditions may alter the relevance of those patterns. Agency itself becomes problematic and remains unthematized. In the American social movement tradition, especially after the 1960s, the emphasis within more radical sectors rests on taking action, largely symbolic, and not with thematizing conditions and reflecting on ideological frameworks as a basis for action. As such, the particular constraints of the U.S. institutional and ideological context are not considered, either in relation to action or theory. What remains are forms and understandings that are ill-suited for the context. NSM theory, interestingly, rationalizes these blockages.

In an effort to demonstrate the noncontestational character of ascribed NSM features, I will focus on several traits of the 1980s and 1990s student movement that raise questions concerning the democratic character and transformative potential of NSMs generally. Based on my own observations as a practitioner within the U.S. student movement from 1984 to

1992, it is my contention that one or more of the earlier cited characteristics (a contradictory stance toward the state, overemphasis on the prefigurative, and an attachment to identity politics) challenges the old paradigm associated with the working-class and anti-imperialist struggles of the late nineteenth and early- to mid-twentieth centuries. Ultimately, these challenges justifiably reflect the inadequacy of the old paradigm as well as changing historical conditions. However, NSM practices among U.S. students present profound political problems that ultimately, I would claim, support anti-democratic, ahistorical, and nonegalitarian tendencies in practice and theory, which do not provide a viable alternative to either dominant arrangements or the problems associated with the old Left paradigm.

PROBLEMS IN FOCUS, FORM, AND AIMS

It is fair to say that the waves of student activism beginning in 1985 did not manifest an easily definable or widely shared understanding of the role of the state in society. NSM theorists offer a variety of post-Marxist paradigms that seek to explain the inferred relationship between the modern state and the emergence of NSMs, as well as to describe NSMs' posture toward the state and its perceived strategic role in the process of transformation. The close association NSMs share with noninstitutional politics (i.e., type of issue addressed and strategy choices) has reinforced a view of them as positing an alternative basis for politics in which radical transformation is neither predicated on working-class interest nor on formal institutional strategies. The lack of state orientation among NSMs, as well as their ascribed middle-class composition, are perceived to underpin a new politics that seeks to reconstitute civil society, away from state and economic control, by "adopting practices that belong to an intermediate sphere between private pursuits and concerns, on the one side, and institutional, state-sanctioned modes of politics on the other."[5] Success, in these terms, is defined in opposition to representative institutions and universal (or shared) values, and relies heavily on the symbolic or rhetorical quality of the demand. As a result, NSMs lack strategies that actually contest state or economic power in any determinate way. In response to various forms of economism and fatalism (the second being the more profound obstacle to organizing young people today), NSM theorists are grappling with the contingent character of current social movements. Unfortunately, the disappearance of state-oriented strategies as well as the obscuring of the accumulation process among social movements has made it difficult, in this case, for the 1980s and early 1990s U.S. student movement to effect centers of power.

With regard to the state, the dominant trend in recent U.S. student activism would seem to support the view that NSMs, at least in rhetoric and in certain intraorganizational practices, reject the idea of the expanded modern state on the grounds that it is inherently oppressive. Yet their reliance on the state at strategic moments reveals an inadequate and contradictory conception of politics and power. The popular student activist paradigm known as "identity politics" fails to distinguish between different types of hierarchies and, as a result, many U.S. student activists (either in practice or rhetoric) see the economy, the state, and what can now be bracketed as "social relations," as equivalent threats to subjectivity. Popular wisdom among this generation of student activists seems to reflect the idea that, for example, the welfare state, class analysis, and the call for a national confederation of student groups into a united block formation are all expressions of dominance. Two exemplary moments in the 1980s and 1990s U.S. student movement illustrate these tendencies.

The Student Anti-Apartheid Movement

In 1966, members of the SNCC attempted to deliver a message to the South African diplomatic mission in New York City. The situation erupted in violence between the SNCC delegation and the mission representatives, and SNCC members were arrested on charges of physical assault.[6] Since that time, the issue of South African liberation has been a constant feature of U.S. student movement politics, although with varying degrees of emphasis and clarity.

During the mid-seventies, under the banner of the African Liberation Support Committee, apartheid South Africa was addressed within the general anti-imperialist framework advanced for Africa as a whole by the ALSC.[7] The period that followed witnessed sporadic protest of the South African regime, almost exclusively coming from the black community, until the South Africa regime's 1977 slaying of prominent national student leader and advocate of Black Consciousness, Steven Biko. Following the death of Biko, U.S. students from Dartmouth and Yale protested their university's complicity in the South Africa regime and called for divestment from companies doing business there. In 1978, according to Keith Jennings, more than 20,000 people, mostly students from historically black colleges, demonstrated against the Davis Cup tennis matches, which included the South African National Team, at Vanderbilt University.[8] Additionally, Catalyst, an anti-racism social action group, sponsored speakers on the issue at campuses nationally beginning in 1977.[9]

The anti-apartheid issue remained a component of U.S. student movement campaigns throughout the period between 1979 and 1983, supported by black student unions, TransAfrica, the American Committee on Africa, and the Washington Office on Africa, as well as white student groups such as the Progressive Student Network. Successful campaigns for university divestment (although in many cases only partial) spawned regional conferences, mainly in the Northeast. But most anti-apartheid organizers agree that 1983 and 1984 were turning points due to the leverage the issue was given by the Rainbow Coalition and the Reverend Jesse Jackson during his 1984 presidential bid. Additionally, the Free South Africa Movement—which organized prominent Civil Rights leaders, mayors, members of Congress, entertainers, and labor and church leaders into an ongoing civil disobedience campaign outside the South Africa Embassy in Washington, D.C.—brought national media attention to the Reagan administration's policy of constructive engagement. Students also played a crucial role in these demonstrations. Most important, however, was that the stepped-up protests in South Africa, led by the ANC, provided world-wide coverage of the South Africa regime's brutal retaliation and imposition of martial law.

The year 1985 stands out in U.S. student movement history because it witnessed the culmination of these many years of activity in an explosion of student-led campaigns against apartheid. There were significant outbursts beginning in February when more than a thousand students joined the ongoing Free South Africa Movement protests (in Washington, D.C.) in celebration of the twenty-fifth anniversary of the U.S. student sit-in movement opposing Jim Crow laws (U.S. apartheid). Other noteworthy events included the March 1985 marking of the Sharpeville Massacre of Atlanta, where fifteen hundred students from historically black colleges demonstrated. In April 1985, Columbia University students, marking the anniversary of Dr. King's assassination, took over a main campus building, renaming it Mandela Hall. Columbia marked the beginning of a tidal wave of campus takeovers,[10] which did not subside until well into 1986 and continued less forcefully into 1987. By 1987, student political action brought 128 schools to pledge to fully (and in some cases partially) divest holdings connected to South Africa. In December 1986, it was estimated that almost $4 billion in investments had been affected.[11] The breadth, diversity, and tactical creativeness of the campus divestment movement brought many previously unacquainted students into contact with one another. It also confronted these students with a host of organizational dilemmas and ideological divisions that existed beneath the thin consensus of opposition to apartheid South Africa. Unprepared and divided, the student anti-apartheid movement was unable to coalesce organizationally at the national level.

During the summer of 1985, the first major conference attempting to give the explosive campus divestment movement some direction took place in Chicago. That meeting foreshadowed many of the problems that continue to affect the U.S. student movement today. Despite the clarion call against apartheid South Africa, the major obstacles to that meeting's success included a clash over the legitimacy of an ongoing national structure; a clash over processes of accountability; and a clash over the legitimacy of multi-racial organizing.

Time and time again, the U.S. student movement has been confronted with making a decision on forming some type of national structure—usually in the form of a coalition around a single issue. In this situation, there was an impulse among some black student leaders, many from the South, to establish an ongoing anti-apartheid *and* anti-racism coalition that would be well-represented in its leadership by those who have historically carried the issue—black students—while also representing, in membership and leadership, committed whites, Latinos, Asian, and Native American students. Such a position assumed the need for national coordination as a strategy to reverse the federal policy dubbed constructive engagement. In this sense, these students sensed the need to go beyond contesting university administrations and believed they could be a force in effecting state power. Secondly, this position also assumed multi-racial organizing as well as accountability in organizational structure, that is, a democratically elected leadership. The proposed name for the coalition was the Student Coalition against Apartheid and Racism (SCAR).

Various elements that participated in this and subsequent meetings opposed the idea of SCAR for various reasons. Some advanced the idea that a national coalition was not necessary, that in fact all that was needed was a loose network. This position was represented by the Progressive Student Network and other already formed groups which, it was later argued, were threatened by the prospect of such an entity. PSN was a Midwest-based, predominantly white organization whose origins were in the Freedom Road Socialist Party, a reinvention of the RYM2, which was a Maoist faction of the late SDS. In response to the difficulty of drawing in young people under Marxist ideology, PSN had already adopted a new social movement strategy nationally, along with consensus-style decision making and voluntary leadership. It should be noted that the objection to consolidating the disparate movement was frequently made on the grounds that those behind the meeting were trying to "take control" of the anti-apartheid movement. Ironically, PSN had been criticized at the outset of the meeting for taking credit in press releases for organizing the meeting. PSN's opposition to a formation was seen by some as self-interested because individual groups enjoy greater autonomy within a network, and this would allow them to recruit new students without being accountable to a larger group.

Other students opposed the forming of a national coalition on the basis that the room's audience was not completely representative of the entire student movement. In this case, the argument was made along regional lines. Any attempt to form an organization, in this view, would be seen as premature due to the fact that many elements would not be represented in the founding. This perspective reflects the emphasis on prefiguring the conditions such an organization would be interested in bringing about socially. Still other students with a black nationalist orientation opposed the formation of a coalition structure on the grounds that there was no need to work with white (or Asian, Native, or Latino) students on any permanent basis. Additionally, there were disagreements over the style of decision making (parliamentarian v. consensus), as well as issues of representation and membership (group representatives v. individual membership base). The only decision arrived at was to have another meeting.

Many of the problems evidenced at the national level had their roots in local antagonisms associated with differences in organizing styles—sometimes framed by student organizers as unacknowledged class and race privilege. As a generalization, white student organizers would demonstrate a preference for "nonhierarchical" structures (no leaders) and consensus-style decision making, whereas black organizers (and other students of color) demonstrated a preference for representative structures and parliamentarian procedures. To complicate matters, not all black student leaders felt a multi-racial coalition, either locally or nationally, was a desirable goal (despite the spontaneous and substantial emergence of white-student participation in the sit-ins). Those students, regardless of racial or ethnic identity, who promoted multi-racial organizing under the anti-apartheid banner, were frequently also advocates of a national coalitional structure with elected leaders and more traditional decision-making processes (majoritarian decision making). These students tended to have a more long-range view of organizing. Keith Jennings, founding member of the Georgia Black Student Association and the Atlanta Student Coalition against Apartheid and Racism, was one of the initiators of the call and expressed this long-range view: "We must take our time in this process of building a viable student organization dedicated to assisting in eliminating apartheid and building a student movement that, in time, could once again have the respect of youth and students throughout the world."[12]

One other difference among elements of the student anti-apartheid movement at this time related to the question of targeting power. Frequently, student campaigns reflected a naiveté about whom or what they were really struggling against (the university governors? the U.S. government? multinational corporations?). As a result, the organizational vehicles that were advocated indicated a partial perspective on power relations. Instead of building a democratic national structure that could interconnect mass mobilizations (directed at both the U.S. government and multinational corporations), a diffuse student movement, successful in many respects, instead relied on scattered local and regional corporate boycotts and a spontaneous campus-by-campus divestment strategy.

Similar experiences on campuses such as Berkeley, Rutgers, and Columbia, foreshadowed the problems of establishing consensus at the national level. Many of these problems can be explained as a complex and non-cohering mix of NSM assumptions and divisions associated with identity politics. In particular, the Berkeley divestment movement serves as a microcosm, in many ways, for the larger themes that inhibited the development of an ongoing national student anti-apartheid movement. In his own words, student organizer Pedro Noguera recounts, for interviewer Tony Vellela, the antagonisms resulting from differences in tactics and strategies:

The first organized event was organized by the African Students Association. Right after that, a group of white students who attended said they wanted to form an organization and they wanted us to work with them. They wanted to form an organization and do a protest. I said we wanted to focus on getting black students more involved. The following week they had a protest, a picket, and things kind of developed from there. They started their own organization . . . and we started our organization. They were basically parallel. Ours was multi-racial, theirs was basically white. They would initiate an action and then it would be up to us to decide whether we would support it or not. At first we would support the actions, even though we didn't like the fact that they weren't well organized, and they didn't focus too much on drawing in more people, or conveying effectively why they were doing the protest to reporters or even the administration. The very first civil disobedience action took place at University Hall in December of 1984, where about 30 people or so were arrested for blockading the entrance. I was one of the people who went inside to present the demands to the administration, but the demands were not worked out ahead of time; they were made up at the time. They also locked arms with each other, which led to many people getting hurt because when the police started prying people off, they were pulling them back. And some people who were not citizens got arrested. From that period, we started having intense discussions and debates over tactics and strategies. And they continued for two years.[13]

One of the more repeated criticisms by black students during the anti-apartheid movement was that white student activists frequently proposed highly symbolic tactics in which each situation was pushed to its most "radical" conclusion—namely confrontation with the police and usually resulting in arrests. Despite the long tradition of civil disobedience associated with the Civil Rights community, white activists frequently depicted black student organizers as being too conservative; in response, black activists felt that many whites lacked organizational discipline and were using arrest tactics indiscriminately without considering the effect— both in terms of the overuse of the tactic as well as the cost to less privileged students. Barbara Ransby of the University of Michigan has stated: "The dynamic of racism in our society is one in which black people have been historically disempowered, and one sort of liberal response has been tokenism, trying to make blacks exactly parallel to a white experience instead of understanding fundamental differences—for example, how black working-class students see being arrested versus how upper-middle-class white students might perceive the same thing."[14]

The question of tactics raises the specter of strategy and theory; here the argument over when to get arrested reveals a broader disagreement—in this case, it appears to be primarily about race and class difference, but this is the danger of identity politics. Upon further analysis the conflict, while certainly experienced as a race and class difference, also reveals a more profound difference in world view. In many ways, these dilemmas represent the clash of two unresolved tendencies belonging to the previous generation: the radical Civil Rights tradition prior to co-optation (represented by the Martin Luther Kings of the Poor People's Movement) on the one hand, versus the more symbolic elements of both the counterculture (Yippie!) and militant black nationalist groupings. While the latter categories encompass very divergent elements, it can be argued that they have three things in common: a rejection of a mass-based united struggle; an anti-statist position; and a rejection (for different reasons) of parliamentary or majoritarian decision-making procedures.

In its 1980s incarnation, symbolic militancy among black students gave way to a logic that included the idea that apartheid was a black issue and therefore whites had no real stake in organizing outside of a minor support role. Such was the case at Rutgers University, although the role divisions occurred informally—the thirty-two-day sit-in comprised primarily whites, and the leadership (who organized the sit-in) was all black except for one seat. Spokesperson Lisa Williamson (also known as Sister Souljah) argued that whites had neither the competency nor the right to make decisions that could affect the lives of black people. In the same vein, black people should not seek leadership on, for example, Central America's issues: "You don't see black students trying to take charge of protests for Nicaragua or El Salvador?"[15] Uncompromising in her rhetoric, she explained the low numbers of black student participation in the sit-in: "Many black students said they were grossed out by the homosexual populace at the sit-in, the uncleanly conditions."[16] Also an active figure at the national level, Lisa Williamson's rhetorical style reverberated and fueled misperceptions and fragmentation.

At such campuses, white students frequently accepted the underlying tenets of identity politics and thus did not have to account for their own organizing tactics. As at Berkeley, two anti-apartheid groups resulted—an ironic commentary, it would seem. As Barbara Ransby has commented:

> It's easy for a lot of whites to not deal with racism and take themselves off the hook by saying "oh yeah, we support black separatism, go over there and do your own thing." It absolves them: they don't have to deal with their own racism, and they don't have to give up any power in their own organization. So what might seem like a progressive position, respecting the autonomy of black political organizations, might also be an excuse for not confronting their own racism.[17]

The primary contradictions between the radical Civil Rights tradition and today's identity politics, as evidenced by the anti-apartheid student movement, brings us back to the three characteristics of NSM outlined as problematic: the opposition to consolidation on the grounds that it is a form of domination indistinguishable from statism or corporatism; the adherence to prefigurative norms such as consensus decision making, a rejection of identifiable structures, the claim that no national organization should be formed until "everyone" is represented (where "everyone" becomes a constantly shifting and indeterminate category); and a rejection of universalist criteria. These three NSM elements represent the movements' unwillingness to link issues to a general program and a refusal to theoretically totalize conditions. Such a posture has become deeply imprinted on the current U.S. student movement. The anti-apartheid movement was in many ways the most promising moment in the current student movement because it presented students with the clearest choices; the student anti-apartheid movement carried the radical Civil Rights tradition into the national student movement more persuasively than any other national student effort to date.

Assumptions within this tradition make it possible to overcome the fragmentation of student politics while providing a framework that honors the validity and strength of non-class-based struggles alongside an analysis of economic relations. While the tradition also carries with it the bifurcated path, the unrealized potential of the early Civil Rights years—in light of co-optation and the slide into symbolic radicalism—also holds the greatest potential for reconsideration and reflection on the interrelation of institutional, cultural, and economic forces. Not incidentally, 1985 provided a unique opportunity for U.S. students to consider these dilemmas within the context of an international movement.

Despite the significant contributions of students in 1985, no ongoing anti-apartheid, anti-racism national organization of young people was developed in this country. Since that time, students have had important opportunities to consolidate their actions, and yet similar obstacles prevented them. Nonetheless, urgency brought the disparate student movement together in a rather unique, albeit short-lived, way during the Gulf War.

National Youth and Student Campaign for Peace in the Middle East

As noted earlier, after the National Student Convention '88, several national student organizations advocating environmental awareness, reproductive rights, and educational rights were formed in its wake. This trend, however, seemed to signal a recognition of the potential power students and youth could command if consolidated. Yet, intergroup coordination remained elusive, with only a minimal amount of communication taking place across specific agenda interests.

In the late summer of 1990, after the Iraqi invasion of Kuwait and the subsequent U.S. military mobilization along the Kuwait border, many U.S. activist groups, while planning their fall agendas, took note of the grave situation. Informal relationships between activists were formed and "what if" plans were discussed. Throughout the fall of 1990, however, no formal discussions occurred between national and regional organizations. Spontaneous anti-war groups were reported to be cropping up all over the country, and this seemed to reflect a previously untapped element of student activism. Not until December of 1990, when representatives of various student organizations attended a meeting organized by peace organizations (such as the Mobilization for Survival), did students discuss the need for a united student strategy and coalition. At the general meeting, a named was picked (National Campaign for Peace in the Middle East) and Sunday, January 26, 1991 was chosen as the date for a national march in Washington, D.C., to protest the war in Iraq. Students decided to meet separately to devise a strategy to mobilize campuses for the march on Washington and for a follow-up meeting on the Sunday following the march.

At the December meeting, various national youth and student organizations were represented including the United States Student Association, the Student Environmental Action Coalition, DSA-YS, PSN, and the Student Action Union, as well as independent activists from Louisiana State University–Baton Rouge and other campus-based anti-war groups. In addition, the "youth" sections of more orthodox socialist parties such as the Socialist Workers Party and the International Socialist Organization were present as well. In addition to mobilizing campuses for the Washington, D.C., march, the idea was floated to organize a national student meeting the day after the march, at which time continued national strategies for students would be decided. Toward that end, organizers present at the meeting set a date for a more representative phone conference call at which time they would decide how to proceed.

Over the course of the next six weeks, more than 130 national, regional, and independent local student and youth activist affiliations signed on to the National Youth and Student Campaign for Peace in the Middle East.

In that short span of time, an office was opened in Washington, D.C., a meeting hall was secured for the January 27 meeting, and seventeen core organizations participated in four conference calls. Problems developed immediately due to the lack of an accountable structure. The campaign had been conceived as an emergency coalition, and therefore few ground rules, outside of opposition to the war, had been established. The breadth of the campaign—ideologically, racially, regionally, its gender balance, and its ability to unite so many disparate agendas (reproductive rights, the environment, anti-racism organizations, lesbian and gay organizations, educational rights groups, etc.) had more to do with the sense of urgency created by the war itself than with any resolution of the types of disagreements that usually mark such meetings. In fact, the campaign was just that—an anti-war campaign and not a real coalition. Disagreement did not really begin to emerge until the agenda for the meeting on January 27 was discussed.

Due to the lack of any organizational structure, the agenda came under attack approximately two weeks before the meeting. Complaints about the process being exclusive and undemocratic abounded. Because all decisions occurred on the phone with as many as seventeen participants and no formal structure, the process was in fact chaotic and determined by individual (group) initiative. The lack of ground rules regarding requirements for participation meant that any individual with persistence could become part of the core decision-making group.

About one week before the scheduled meeting in Washington, D.C., new guidelines were announced, limiting participation to youth and student organizations of a national or regional basis, as well as other nonaffiliated campus and high school organizations. Any group meeting these requirements could participate in all decision making by designating two representatives, who would together make up a coordinating committee. Sectarian party organizations without formal youth sections were angered and subsequently proved problematic at the meeting.

The agenda for the meeting was to be finalized in a midnight meeting on January 25, in which the then–fifty-seven affiliated organizations would meet for the first time and approve the agenda. With little disagreement, the January 27 meeting agenda was set, with goals to include the approval of five demands (withdraw all troops, end all occupations, end the poverty draft, end racism, develop a sustainable energy policy) and uniting for a day of youth and student action on February 21. The list of demands demonstrates the symbolic function of social movements in the United States: Without a focused institutional objective or point of entry, students, in an effort to be "representative" and therefore "legitimate," attached a list of demands across a wide spectrum of social movement concerns that were strictly rhetorical. Conversely, decision-making procedures within the group became a concern. More debate occurred over *how* to vote than over the merits of the strategies proposed. In lieu of real power, significance was attached to procedures that participants could control; in essence, process took precedence over substance. Voting, it was ultimately decided, would occur within prescribed regions on a one-person-one-vote, majoritarian, basis.

On Sunday, January 27, an amazing fifteen hundred students showed up for the meeting representing an additional seventy-three student and youth organizations. In addition, obstructionist elements (Lyndon LaRouche associates and the International Revolutionary Workers League) attended. The loosely knit coordinating committee was overwhelmed with complaints from the floor. In a fashion, epitomizing the prefigurative emphasis on direct democracy, new participants had difficulty accepting an already established agenda. The floor erupted into spontaneous proposals for a new agenda; some groupings opposed the idea of a coordinating committee and proposed a phone and computer network of all participants instead. The 51-percent approval rule was challenged in favor of unanimous consensus or two-thirds approval (being mindful that the room was filled with 1,500 strangers, more or less). The weak coordinating committee regrouped and after an hour recess came back and suggested the floor break up into regions, at which time preassigned moderators were instructed to try and get what they could out of the agenda.

In the end, the National Student and Youth Campaign for Peace in the Middle East accomplished its original goals in adopting four of the five proposals in the assigned regions, all by slim majorities. Fatigued and demoralized, the core organizations that were really holding the campaign together were too exhausted by the event and its aftermath to oversee the February 21 day of coordinated action. Because of both media bias and the students' lack of coordination, sporadic reports came in of campus protests that day, but the effect in no way appeared national. With the abrupt ending of the war, the campaign never met again—not even to assess its organizing efforts. Ties were immediately broken at the war's "end."

The most distinguishing feature of this organizing drive was the success, however brief, of so many groups coming together even for one meeting, thus indicating a substantially more developed national anti-war base among students than at a comparable time during the Vietnam War. This, however, was offset by the lack of desire to form an identifiable organizing structure. Issues of democratic accountability plagued the campaign before and during the meeting. The demands of many participants for an even less formalized and more indeterminate structure made it nearly impossible to proceed.

In both the anti-apartheid movement and the anti-Gulf War effort, the U.S. student movement opted for local, and in some cases regional, formations broken down along single-issue interests. Group autonomy at the base has been perceived as excluding representation on a national level. Internal demands for unanimous agreement in the form of consensus decision making at the local level has made it difficult for local groups to relate to national representative structures in which modified forms of parliamentary process are more wieldy. The exception to this stance was evident only in local groups with a more working-class student base who preferred modified parliamentary process over consensus as consensus requires time that many students balancing work and school simply do not have. But beyond its problems over process, the new student movement lacked strategic clarity about who it was challenging, how it should challenge opponents, and whether it should do so in a unified formation. Student movement demands in the 1980s and 1990s frequently contradict their anti-statist stance (e.g., Money for AIDs, Not for War; Abortion on Demand; Free Education for All; Healthcare Not Warfare). Additionally, the practice of identity politics made it difficult to appeal across single-issue divides and convince younger activists of their stake in a variety of issues.

As representative of the profile depicted by NSM theorists, the 1980s and early 1990s student movement was made up of small, localized (campus-based) grouping that emphasized issues of autonomy, identity, and the attendant concerns with direct democracy. When confronted with legitimate cause, even urgent cause, for consolidation, the recent student movement in the United States was unable, or unwilling, to discover the means or the motivation for such a move. Consolidation in some manner, I would argue, was a political requirement for effectiveness; this is borne out by the alternative route, which, while preserving autonomy, resulted in the petering-out of local formations across a wide spectrum of issues. Additionally, no new efforts aimed at increasing national coordination and shaping a student rights agenda nationally has occurred since the close of the Gulf War. At time of press, various national campus-based efforts—such as

United Students Against Sweatshops—show renewed energy as well as promise. Nationally oriented groups that survived are those that are styled along interest-group lines, like the United States Student Association and the student sections of larger "parent" organizations such as the Public Interest Research Group, the National Abortion Rights Action League, and the National Organization for Women. The loss of momentum is staggering. While students may not be expected to resolve the theoretical conundrum left over from the sixties, an inability to navigate the terrain in any sustainable organizational form suggests that the possibility for resolution and innovation has narrowed.

The unresolved dilemmas in ideology and organizational forms stemming from repertoires of the sixties are now compounded by an increasing emphasis on identity and autonomy from the state in an era of contradictory hegemonic alignments. The political retrenchment of U.S. social movements in the 1990s is particularly ironic given the consolidation of conservative forces at the local, national, and global levels, both politically and economically. In effect, social movements in the United States are ill-equipped to engage in real political power struggles, as evidenced by the paralyzing debates within the anti-apartheid and anti-Gulf War student coalitions. That turf has been effectively conceded to interest groups that, as a matter of institutional disposition, do not engender democratic participation and are substantively constrained by liberalism. Only the WTO/Anti-globalization movement shows significantly counter to this trend.

The constraints of the American system can be deciphered from the debates within social movements. And while financial resources are certainly one constraint, social movement dilemmas are not centrally connected to limited resources, as RM theorists would argue. The problems that exist in and around the question of resources are far more profound. Many NSM theorists argue that the dilemmas I describe are not really dilemmas at all; indeed, they are contestational responses to a new era of "post-industrialism." But, as I have argued, these "new" social movement features can be exposed within the American context as neither contestational nor determined. What appears as new in the American context can be seen as the unconscious internalization of institutional and ideological constraints on those movements seeking political and economic equality.

In particular, "new" social movement forms and focuses testify to the political and ideological basis of movements, delimited within a process of accumulation that generates social and political inequality. As such, it is no longer satisfactory to thematize the production process, or an indistinguishable "bureaucratization" process as some would have it, as determinant of social movement forms. To do so is to miss the institutional and ideological character of social movement repertoires. In doing so, both scholars and participants neglect agency and consign movements to forms that are ineffective at generating substantial change or challenge.

U.S. movements are particularly ineffective at generating contestational strategies as a result of their adherence to nonreflexive ideological practices. NSM theory, because of its assumptions, fails to grasp the relations between national ideological and institutional contexts in conditioning social movement behavior. Likewise, actual movements, instead of viewing the bifurcated U.S. movement history of collapse v. integration as fundamentally political and ideological in nature, and something over which they might have some control, instead raise the rhetorical stakes as if a purer, more disciplined adherence to the prefigurative norms would increase their effectiveness. In this sense, both NSM theory and NSM practice diminish the theoretical control and *obligations* of movement participants.

The practical realities of NSMs require that any theoretical explanation confront the difficulties associated with the forms in various institutional contexts. Knowing that the forms themselves vary in their styles and *impact,* depending on the national context, should highlight for any theoretical explanation the *political* nature of social movements. In this sense, the relationship between economic, institutional, and ideological spheres must be conceived from a *political* standpoint. It follows, then, that agency—the self-conscious recognition of participants—is crucial to any given outcome.

NOTES

1. Unpublished letter to NSAC office. Copy given to Rutgers University activists in January 1987 (Student Action Union Archive, Alexander Library, Rutgers University).
2. Abbie Hoffman, unpublished letter to student.
3. Tony Vellela, *New Voices* (Boston: South End Press, 1988), p. 236.
4. Ray Davis, "Grab Education, My Children," *CrossRoads*, n. 21 (May 1992), p. 5.
5. Offe, p. 820.
6. Keith Jennings, unpublished paper, "The Issue of Apartheid and the U.S. Student Movement: Focus on the Role and Challenge of African-American Students," delivered at Atlanta University Center, Atlanta, Georgia (Sept. 25, 1985), p. 3.

7. Ibid. The ALSC was responsible for organizing the "largest anti-imperialist demonstration dedicated to African liberation to date," in which 80,000 people marched in Washington, D.C.

8. Ibid., p. 4.

9. Vellela, *New Voices*, p. 19.

10. Campuses included such diverse institutions as Yale, Harvard, the entire University of California system, Rutgers, Univ. of Wyoming, Cornell, Ohio Wesleyan, Berea College, Spellman, Grinnell, Penn State, Texas Christian, Vanderbilt, Purdue, University of Washington–Seattle, Atlanta University, the SUNY system, and many more.

11. American Committee of Africa report, "Divestment Action on South Africa by U.S. Colleges and Universities," December 1986.

12. Jennings, p. 10.

13. Vellela, p. 88.

14. Ibid., p. 97.

15. Lisa Williamson, quoted in *The Daily Targum*, Rutgers University, May 8, 1986, p. 3.

16. Ibid.

17. Vellela, p. 98.

PART THREE

Conclusions

Chapter Six

Prospects for a More Reflexive Movement Ideology

Both the social movements of the 1960s and the 1980s U.S. student movement confirm certain "new" social movement trends described by NSM theorists. At the same time, I have called into question the theoretical suggestion that these characteristics are sufficiently accounted for by reference to systemic processes alone. In addition, I have criticized the ascribed efficacy of the new forms on centers of power. Despite the validity of the descriptions, I have argued that a more empirical eye on contemporary social movements underscores the significant influence of national ideological and institutional traditions on the new forms—traditions that can more or less constrain the democratic character of, and options available to, actual movements. In cases like the United States where institutional access and ideological traditions are narrow, the development of a reflexive ideology on the part of social movement participants becomes more pressing. That is to say, the potential for transformation of the status quo is not directly linked to NSMs qua NSMs, but to participants' self-conscious understanding of systemic and contingent processes in relation to generalizable interests and democratic procedures aiming for realization.

Throughout this work I have been critical of the generally optimistic assessment of these movements shared by those I have labeled the New and Post Modernity theorists of NSMs. In particular, I have been critical of the tendency to overdraw the structural/systemic forces in such a way that both the agency of participants and the political preconditions for collective expression are rendered either invisible or thematically inconsequential. The overdrawn systemic claims and the optimism, I contend, are linked by an unacknowledged desire to ensure progress. Likewise, NSM theory has generally failed to emphasize the role of institutional and ideological contexts in the rise and effects of social movements. In an odd pairing of overly determinant systemic explanations with an underdetermined symbolic politics, political processes and ideology are underplayed. As a result, a problem arises in which NSM forms are mistakenly embraced as automatic, thus obscuring the contingent yet necessary role movements themselves must play in developing a persuasive ideological response to systemic and institutional constraints on substantive democracy. NSM theory offers movements little criteria for evaluating their shortcomings and failures. Amid the theorizing, reflexivity, a most fundamental aspect of informed agency, is diminished or lost.

But of course reflexivity too requires normative commitments and purposeful action in order to become something more than a term. Self-conscious, critical reflection must be aimed at those aspects of social and political life that restrain or threaten substantive equality and accountability—both economic and political. Given the significant emptying of these qualities from state functions, the inspiration for their revival, if it is to arise, must come from social movements. In this sense, the norms and procedures once attached to the liberal state, however formally or superficially, are significantly detached and must be reanchored in institutional practice if anything akin to democracy will survive the era.

The degree to which social movements can in fact, and not just symbolically, reassert those values and practices in a new context of global capitalism and waning state controls is the degree to which the suppressed, but more egalitarian, inheritance of liberalism might come to the surface. From the perspective of poor people worldwide, NSMs must be willing to think about and deal with concrete power—both institutional and economic. Such a position requires more than a posture.

COMMUNICATIVE ACTION REVISITED: TURNING ABSTRACTION INTO NEW SOCIAL MOVEMENT PRACTICE

If, as is the case with much of NSM theory, the context of action is thematized in such a way that it is primarily circumscribed by structural (economic, technological) forces, not only are false conclusions drawn as to the nature of NSM forms, but the degree of agency open to the actor is significantly underplayed. In response, in chapter 2, I suggested that the work of Jurgen Habermas provides a general framework in which NSMs may be conceived so as to avoid both false optimism and its consequence, fatalism.

While providing absolutely no guarantees, Habermas's view of social movements as a potential source of communicative action (thus resuscitating the critical public function of the old public sphere) depends almost entirely on the reflexive adoption (both procedurally and normatively) by participants of the processes he identifies with communicative action. But, as I suggested at the end of chapter 2, while Habermas's theory of modernization provides for a differentiated view of reason (suggesting that NSMs are uniquely capable of reflecting critically on their context), his particular account does not thematize the different ways in which the state and the accumulation process might present themselves in various national contexts so as to further constrain or ease the potential for communicative action. That it is possible to do this without contradicting his most basic assumptions makes Habermas's frame most encouraging.

Habermas's account of social movements as potential arenas of communicative action emphasizes the need for a critical capacity, a rational process, and a normative or ideological orientation for the recovery of democratic practice. In order, however, for communicative action to be operationalized within social movements, public sphere obstacles stemming from the accumulation process and the political and institutional arena must be simultaneously thematized and strategically reformed. Social movements therefore must be able to coherently move between strategic and radical modes. Communicative action, it would seem, requires ideological development along these lines for its realization. Below I suggest approaches to thinking about the accumulation process and the institutional context that I believe are, in a very practical sense, useful for social movements in this regard. But first let me sketch the way that communicative action might impact the organizational and ideological pitfalls of actual NSMs in America.

In the previous chapter I suggested that the U.S. student movement of the 1980s was in many respects typical of the kinds of problems haunting NSMs in the United States There and elsewhere I have suggested that NSM ideology and practice in the United States suggests three things: a contradictory stance toward the state; an overemphasis on the prefigurative; and the replacement of a failed Marxist teleology with existential concerns that conflate economic, political and cultural forces. It has been my basic concern here that such an ideological combination favors expression over reflexivity, identity over solidarity, and arbitrariness over binding norms. In both a micro and macro sense, each of these tendencies mitigates against the development of a critical mass public capable of mobilizing against democratic threats; more narrowly, each limits the potential for communicative action.

These three tendencies, more or less pronounced in various social movements of the eighties and nineties, owe much of their shape to the divorce between radical and institutional approaches following the post–World War II context. NSMs in the 1980s were weakened due to a reliance on ideological postures generated in the later part of the 1960s, *without a reflexive awareness of the institutional limits that favored these postures in the first place.* Ultimately they were unable to navigate the political landscape in ways that their relative numbers were felt. While important battles were certainly won (e.g., stemming the tide of nuclear power, the slowing of U.S. support and involvement with antidemocratic regimes such as El Salvador and South Africa, etc.), the ever Right-ward political realignment in state, national, and international politics, and the further dismantling of the moderate liberal welfare state in a pernicious era of global capitalism, demonstrate NSMs' relative weakness.

That social discontent expresses itself, as Habermas puts it, along the seams between system and lifeworld, suggests that political institutions are, at best, distorted institutions of public expression. But this is less a prescription than a diagnosis. If NSMs appear along the seams, their potential rests in redirecting systemic processes through institutional means. Far from conceding the political, NSMs must capture the political in ways that promote accountability and the general welfare. This, I've suggested, relies on reflexively thematizing their position in relation to political and economic processes and institutions. At the same time, a critical understanding of global economic processes and national political processes is a necessary but insufficient condition for sustained NSM activity. This generalized awareness must be reworked into a persuasive movement ideology that links social crises to economic and institutional reform in a manner that, in keeping with Habermas's descriptions, uphold reason, accountability, and fairness. This, as I have tried to demonstrate in the previous chapter, cannot be accomplished while relying on the so-called prefigurative decision-making processes, identity frames and localist fetish so characteristic of the new movements.

Something akin to constitutionally established procedures ensuring accountability (and recall) must bind participants. Expressive, symbolic, and identity-based modes (or what Habermas calls "dramaturgic" modes) may be powerful tactics, but they are inherently flawed as the groundwork for concrete struggles for democracy. While under their sway, not only are disparate social movements largely unable to cohere themselves organizationally, but more fundamentally, they cannot talk across "experiences." Indeed, while emerging in arenas apart from the state, the critical posture of social movements must reaffirm, on the most local level, a respect for procedures—ensuring reciprocity, accountability, and accessibility. But for this to be meaningful, organizational commitments to democratically accountable procedures must avoid the formalism of so much bad liberalism. This may emerge from combining an inward *normative* focus with an outward *strategic* focus on the economic-resource hindrances to a truly accessible public sphere. For contemporary social movements, this can only take the form of a commitment to what Stephen Bronner has called a *class ethic*. In today's environment, this requires that actual movements must undertake a pragmatic emphasis on linking disparate issues and identity claims by way of a class ethic. This move may offer some guidance in turning *communicative action* into something useful.

THE ACCUMULATION PROCESS AND NSM IDEOLOGY: STEPHEN BRONNER'S CLASS ETHIC

NSMs have confirmed the long-standing criticism that orthodox Marxism mistakenly relies on the economy rather than politics for fundamental change. Nonetheless, for the great (European) socialist movements of the nineteenth and early-twentieth centuries, socialism was largely a political and ideological affair. That is to say, the apparent success of historic socialist movements was not really a function of the structural determinism suggested by Marxism, but instead a reflection of the way economic interests and institutional concerns were blended in a persuasive ideological appeal to the working class. Indeed, the eventual failure of socialist movements, it can be argued, resulted from the inability of movements to recognize this fundamentally ideological and political nature of the "class struggle."

While it can certainly be said that Marx's teleology has been proven bankrupt, the same cannot be said about his descriptions of the accumulation process and its undermining effects on liberalism's democratic promise. As Habermas's work demonstrates, the shattered unity between theory and practice resulting from the collapsed teleology does not also necessarily (1) result in an inability to thematize the impact of the accumulation process on politics; (2) entail a rejection of all possible conceptions of universal interest; or (3) jettison the theoretical possibility of viewing particular socioeconomic contradictions (rather than postmodern "antagonisms") as potentially open to institutional resolutions. The rejection of these considerations is often characteristic of many NSMs and much of NSM theory.

Indeed, in the American context, as I have argued, the Lockian liberal attachment to capitalism and the Federalist designs aimed at restricting "factions" prove to be the crucial clues to the puzzling lack of effectiveness characteristic of American NSMs. In the American context, an ideological veil has been cast over the relationship between institutional and economic interest and as a result, social movements here have historically been unable to account for their marginalization in the political process. As argued in chapter 4, these constraining foundations of American politics have only been exacerbated by the decline of accountability in an era of interest group liberalism. The history of post–World War II challenges demonstrates that the desire of some social movement participants to retain a radical stance in an era of decreasing accountability could not be met without sacrificing, in Abbie Hoffman's words, precision for suggestion. The current situation in America, declining accountability *and* receding welfare functions, only heightens the need to thematize the impact of the accumulation process generally and in relation to NSM aims. Here the work of Stephen Bronner is quite useful.

STEPHEN BRONNER'S "CLASS IDEAL"

In his book *Socialism Unbound*, Stephen Bronner proposes a response to the indeterminacy resulting from the break between theory and practice. Sober and practical, the socialist response for Bronner requires the development of a class ethic that, while contingent and open to critical evaluation, incorporates universalist presuppositions as a basis for judgment and unified action. Recognizing the overlapping character of the economic, the political, and the cultural levels of society, Bronner nonetheless highlights the practical need for "rough heuristic distinctions." Diverse NSMs, from a practical interest, should seek to overcome the fragmentation through the development of an ethic that validates social and political demands yet also retains a "structural perspective critical of capitalist society." Bronner argues:

> The point, then, is to formulate unifying principles that speak to each of the composite groups and give priority to none, but which can also confront the contradictions of the existing accumulation process. . . . A socialist political theory must subsequently develop an integrated perspective that can combine formal equality for all groups with the interests specific to the working people within each.[1]

For Bronner, the question remains: From where do these unifying principles gain their meaning? The real and legitimate demands for social and political autonomy and control will always be confronted with intragroup class divisions; a review of NSMs from a socialist perspective requires the reassertion of the substantive aims of socialist democracy because "all who sell their labor power do not have an interest in rendering capital democratically accountable." [2] In this sense, the structural moment of expropriation, now divorced from the politics of a labor movement, is reformulated as an ideological and political moment termed by Bronner a *class ideal*. Contingent and speculative, class no longer has political significance merely due to empirical definition or structural location, but instead must be articulated practically and theoretically as an organizing principle *within social movements* whose demands for substantive democracy are otherwise universally unrealizable. Bronner summarizes:

> A new perspective predicated on a socialist ethic will then necessarily appear far more modest than the old. More than that, it will stand in direct contrast to the political optimism and sense of scientific certainty which played such an important role in orthodox Marxism. But recognizing the contingent character of a socialist future is only to admit that history has not conformed to Marx's teleological predictions and that no party or movement any longer incarnates the truth of historical development. The existing conditions of political fragmentation among workers and postmodern confusion among radical intellectuals are impossible to avoid. Thus, strangely enough, the idealist interpretation of the socialist project becomes justified on materialist ground.[3]

Bronner's contribution makes two assumptions with which some NSM theorists, like Laclau and Mouffe, would disagree. For Bronner, there is an explicit assumption of intersubjective competence: that any subject is capable of rendering "a judgment on how any given choice contributes to the formation of an emancipated order" using a common criterion such as the class ideal. For Laclau and Mouffe as well as for many NSM participants, the assumption of intersubjective competence is rendered irrelevant as a result of investments in radical subjectivity either in the form of postmodern theories or the practice of identity politics, which suggest "truth," or knowledge, is experientially based.

Most importantly, Bronner's strategy assumes the desire for democratically accountable structures, within both NSM groupings and state institutions. The conception of the class ideal would assist NSMs in creating the unity needed to confront and reconstitute centers of power, such as party structures, and representative institutions at all levels of political life. In culturalist theories like Laclau and Mouffe's, as well as in the actual NSMs discussed in previous chapters, a commitment to unified mass organizations is rare; in this sense, the prefigurative has greater priority than actual institutional reform. Of course, it is in this light that the limited force of an ethic is made evident. Bronner's class ethic, while contingent, merely underscores my argument that social movements—their form, aims, and focus—are largely political and ideological in nature. Bronner's formulation can only serve as a guide for reflexive movement ideology; it cannot guarantee success.

POLITICAL CONTEXT AND NSM STRATEGY: PIVEN AND CLOWARD REVISED

In chapter 1 I was careful to set aside the work of those associated with the "political process approach" to social movement studies. There I suggested that while often lumped in with the Resource Mobilization approach, the work of scholars like Charles Tilly, Doug McAdam, and Frances Fox Piven and Richard Cloward offers a sophisticated analysis of the interplay between radical movements and the political institutional context. This approach relates the rise and degree of impact of radical social movements to, in a phrase, the disequilibrium of political arrangements usually in the context of economic trends. Like Resource Mobilization (RM), the logic of movement formation and impact can be gauged in relation to resources—in this case the defining resource is opportunity generated by unstable political arrangements. Able to capitalize on an atmosphere of electoral instability, social movements, in this outlook, have a chance of being heard and even gaining limited concessions. My criticism then and now is not that such descriptions are not empirically verifiable or even fairly predictive, but that ultimately such a framework ties social movement function to the logic of the political process and, as a result, to large-scale economic trends. This, I'd like to argue, is true of the work of Piven and Cloward, who suggest that even under the best circumstances, radical demands are met with "conciliatory pronouncements." In other words, there is an embedded assumption that social movements cannot self-consciously generate opportunities, nor are they able to radically alter electoral arrangements in such a way that challenges the instrumentalism of the political process. Movements, therefore, are best at being disrupters when opportunity strikes. Radicals are interlopers, capable of denting the tank. While exceedingly sober, it is a vision, however, that flattens the one strength of NSMs in our era: the anticipatory impulse of the "great refusal."

This may appear an odd line of critique given my extensive argument here that radical social movements are in dire need of paying more attention to the institutional context. But, in a certain sense, I am much closer to and rely quite substantially on the understanding of the political process presented in the work of Piven and Cloward. Yet, my argument is that the political process, dominated as it is by the instrumentalism of, in the case of the United States, interest-group liberalism, must be viewed by movements as a pivotal target for democratic transformation, and not mere disruption. When the relationship between the political process and structural or systemic tendencies is viewed as dynamic and not determinant as is the case here, then the political process remains open to change in any number of directions. This observation means that theorists and participants alike must consider the possibility that developments might also bring about a complete closure of the assumed limits and opportunities for social movement impact thematized in the political process literature. In this sense, the state must become a target *for dramatic democratic transformation if the critical role of radical social movements is to be preserved at all.* This kind of transformation cannot be accomplished if social movements assign themselves to the role of interloper.

While the political process approach understands the impact of existing institutional patterns on social movements more keenly than any other current framework, it does not sufficiently grasp the tentative ideological relationship between movement and the context. Indeed, to the extent that critical consciousness is posited as a direct function of events largely beyond the control of agents, the real threats to movement potential remain unthematized. Movement ideology is rendered functional, not reflexive. In a similar vein, and perhaps of more concern, is the way social movements may be caught off guard as waning state controls on the accumulation process and diminished electoral controls eclipse the limited potential of movements altogether. In this sense the transformative potential of social movements becomes linked to jettisoning the deterministic elements of analysis and, in their place, highlighting the ideological responsibilities of social movements in our era.

A more reflexive, critical awareness of the political process on the part of social movements can more adequately provide a basis for movements themselves to understand their location and accept their responsibility to become reflexive in their strategies, organizational forms, and tactics. Below I argue that in the American context, a *critical appropriation* of the political-process approach, evident in the work of Piven and Cloward, can contribute to a reflexive understanding of the institutional context as both restraint on and target for fundamental institutional and political change.

Much like Charles Tilly, the work of Piven and Cloward evidences a degree of critical distance on the logic of collective action that goes beyond much in the RM paradigm. This flows from the perspective on the rise of the nation–state in relation to economic developments; indeed the political process is defined in the context of the nation–state. The nation–state is both a result of and a restraint upon modern social movements. As the defining element in the rise and outcome of social movements, the emergence of the nation–state, with its attendant claims to represent large numbers of people through some form of representative institutions, stimulated groups of people with little formal power to seek greater access and control over state powers. Tilly defines social movements as:

A sustained series of interactions between power holders and persons successfully claiming to speak on behalf of a constituency lacking formal representation, in the course of which those persons make publicly visible demands for changes in the distribution or exercise of power and back those demands with public demonstrations of support.[4]

Social movements for Tilly, it follows, cannot exist where no state authorities exist. By definition, social movements are *national* social movements and are labeled accordingly. For Tilly, the role of the national political process in conditioning and mediating social movement demands is apparent. It is fundamental. For Tilly, however, the political process encompasses more than just a strict formal institutional boundary. In responding to the characterizations of social movements as forms of unconventional behavior (another tenet of the Collective Behavior model), Tilly says, "Movements actually stem from durable features of the American social structure and politics rather than from timeless regularities in the behavior of unconventional groups of a certain kind."[5] Social movements, then, are seen as expressions of shared interest among groups occupying a disadvantaged position in the overall institutional (structural) context. This is precisely the kind of emphasis on context that RM theory eschews. Like Tilly, Piven and Cloward perceive the causes of social movement activity to be largely political. But in their view of what comprises the political context, Piven and Cloward make explicit provisions for the forces of the economy and ideology in shaping and mediating social movements.

In their widely acclaimed book, *Poor People's Movements*, Frances Fox Piven and Richard Cloward forward a compelling thesis about the structural possibilities of poor people in the United States to effect political change through social movements. It is their general view that the institutional arrangements of society (including work, family, community, and state power) preclude the poor from protest on their own behalf by effectively enforcing the dominant ideological view that poverty is caused by a lack of talent. Additionally, those same institutional arrangements render the poor structurally vulnerable to the penalties of challenge, thus reinforcing docility. In their book, *Why American's Don't Vote*, for example, Piven and Cloward offer an explanation as to how voter registration processes and the two-party system, as traditional electoral routes of expression, are biased against the poor. Nevertheless, in *Poor People's Movements,* Piven and Cloward look at four instances in America history in which the poor have, in fact, risen above these biases and protested on their own behalf.

The question they pose and seek to answer is: Under what conditions do the lower classes become defiant? In other words, *why* and *when* do the poor engage in social movement activity? They suggest that the lower classes engage in protest under conditions of rapid economic change (in conformance with either James C. Davis's "rising expectations" theory or the classic Marxist notion of immiseration). Moreover, they argue that the lower classes engage in social movement activity when the "regulatory capacities" of the structures of daily life are weakened as a result of dramatic shifts in economic conditions.[6]

Piven and Cloward claim that the electoral-representative system is "the principal structuring institution" of social movement activity among the lower classes. But not because voting offers an avenue of expression for the poor. Instead they suggest,

> It is usually when unrest among the lower classes breaks out of the confines of electoral procedures that the poor may have some influence, for the instability and polarization they threaten to create by their actions in the factories or in the streets may force some response from electoral leaders.[7]

Moreover, Piven and Cloward contend that one of the first signs of discontent in the United States is "usually a sharp shift in traditional voting patterns" either in the form of party defection or voter attrition.[8] Rapid economic change, it follows, induces an insecure electoral environment thus accelerating competition for votes. Accordingly, the atmosphere is then conducive to potential gains by the poor (or, it would follow, any group of "nonvoters"). They state:

> These early signs of political instability ordinarily prompt efforts by contending political leaders to placate the defecting groups, usually at this stage with conciliatory pronouncements. The more serious the electoral defections, or the keener the competition among political elites, the more likely that such symbolic appeasements will be offered.[9]

Piven and Cloward, as well as Tilly, approach social movement studies from the standpoint that the interplay between the economy and institutional arrangements are fundamental in the rise and outcomes of social movements. For Piven and Cloward, shifts in the economy affect electoral environments. While their work focuses on the economic, ideological, and institutional position of the poor within such a context, their more general claim is akin to that of E. E. Schattshneider: a socialization of conflict (in this case, social movement activity) is more likely to occur and succeed in an atmosphere of competition between the two parties. The threat of action by nonvoters creates insecurity within the system and heightens fear of a sudden expansion of the scope of conflict. Piven and Cloward argue that competition among the parties is created when the economy makes sudden shifts.

In such an approach, we see the interplay of economic and institutional arrangements, and collective actors. The theoretical grounding for such a view is Marxian in its roots, though Piven and Cloward would reject the teleological assumptions of orthodox Marxism. Their ability to tie various levels of social life together—the group, political institutions, and the economy—derives from what they term a dialectical analysis:

> Movements are not forged merely by willing or thinking or arguing them into existence. Proletarian movements, Marx said, are formed by a dialectical process reflecting the institutional logic of capitalist arrangements. The proletariat is a creature, not of communists, but of capital and the conditions of capitalist production. . . . Of course, historical developments frustrated Marx's prediction: expanding capitalist production did not create a revolutionary proletariat. Still, the basic model of dialectical analysis underlying the failed prediction—the idea that the struggles of ordinary people are both formed by and directed against institutional arrangements—is correct.[10]

Piven and Cloward's approach to social movements emphasizes institutional patterning as a context out of which grievances arise and are simultaneously constrained. Their terminology may be misleading: by institutional arrangements, Piven and Cloward mean roughly work, family, community, and state structures. Each of these spheres is shaped by the "conditions of capitalist productions." This claim, that the actions of movement participants are prodded by economic conditions, accounts for, although does not elaborate on, the issue of agency. Possibilities for resistance and reflexive ideology must be thematized in ways that allow for some autonomy from the conditioning effects of economic and institutional forces—otherwise how is challenge possible in the first place? Are these movements consciously conceived of by participants? To what extent does the ideological consciousness of the participants affect outcomes? And, most importantly, can participants generate new institutional patterns over which they may exercise greater control? Or must their activation be determined upon economic up or downturns? These are the fundamental concerns, I contend, for current social movement theory.

Tilly and Piven and Cloward reject the determinism of orthodox Marxism, but the dialectical frame for social relations clearly retains its Marxist cast. This tension between a rejection of the Marxian teleology ("the failed prediction") and the embracing of the dialectical method is the cause for residues of functionalism that mark their thesis. At the same time, they offer sound explanations as to why some movements succeeded (in their terms), and others did not. But all the movements under consideration are tied to economic practices and electoral arrangements largely pre-dating the period in which significant new social movement trends begin to emerge.

While Piven and Cloward's framework retains a high level of internal coherence in applied cases, conditions today suggest that the kind of economic shifts and the political response envisioned there are increasingly autonomous. (And perhaps they always have been!) It is my argument that a social movement is primarily an ideological affair irrespective of economic ups and downs. But this is not to say that as fundamentally ideologically based efforts, systemic and institutional processes are irrelevant. Quite the opposite. It is just the manner in which these relations are thematized in the work of Piven and Cloward that requires revision for social movements in our era.

Piven and Cloward emphasize the interplay between the economy and institutional arrangements as fundamental. They refer to their own theoretical approach as dialectical and suggest that economic shifts and institutional patterns condition the choices made by social movements. At the same time, Piven and Cloward tend to underemphasize the ability of social movement participants to generate possibilities themselves: "Movements are not forged merely by willing or thinking or arguing them into existence. . . . The proletariat is a creature, not of communists, but capitalist arrangements." [11]

Dependent on shifts in the economy that generate institutional instability, social movements in Piven and Cloward are creatures of economic fluctuation. While originating largely outside the institutional context (because of exclusive structures), social movements can make demands on institutions in an electoral climate shaken into competition by rapid economic shifts. The secret to social movement success is their threat as blocs of *nonvoters* who may potentially disturb the balance of power assumed by the two parties.

I agree with Piven and Cloward that the American institutional context is characterized by a limited electoral-representative system marked by a belabored voter-registration process and noncompetitive parties. [12] And while I also agree that movements have historically had influence on parties under rare circumstances of party competition induced by sudden developments, I do not agree that those developments are always economic. Political crises, such as the Vietnam War, can also induce competition between the parties and gain leverage for social movements. But most importantly, it is what movements *do* with that climate that determines outcomes. This is a point often neglected by Piven and Cloward who, despite their penetrating analysis of the role of institutional patterning on social movement formation, tend to leave the role of agency (e.g., reflexivity) unexplored.

Indeed, one of their tenets is that social movements should remain social movements outside the electoral-representative system and fulfill their function as pressure groups instead of consolidating into a third party. This is perhaps my greatest criticism of their work. If discontent is connected to exclusion from the electoral-representative system, it seems crucial that social movements transform that system so as to provide greater access and accountability. This, in my view, can be accomplished only through the consolidation of social movements into a significant electoral block that simultaneously seeks institutional reform while advancing the substantive sociopolitical demands of the base. Here a democratic confederation of the social movement base with parliamentarian capabilities optimizes the potential for impact.

It is essential that social movements in our era reflexively consider the impact of large-scale economic developments and institutional patterns on their goals so that effective challenges can be mounted. In this sense, by dropping the determinism of Piven and Cloward's arguments, we are left with incredibly insightful descriptions of the tendency of social movements to gain leverage in a context of electoral instability. And indeed, this history is crucial for social movements in our era because the restrictive logic of the American political process is largely captured there. But what is more important is that social movements comprehend that electoral instability is not tied functionally to economic developments. Yes, a climate of electoral competition is conducive to social movement impact, but equally important is the understanding that competition can be generated by social movements even during periods of so-called economic stability. It is also important to understand that such an entree is not an opportunity to repeat the cycle of bargaining, concessions, and betrayals endemic to interest-group liberalism, but is instead an invitation to advance radical demands in conjunction with electoral and related institutional reforms that will expand social movement impact. At such a juncture, significant challenge is possible. But for the threat to be sustainable, disparate social movements would already be ideologically coordinated around the class ethic and simultaneously committed to a democratically structured confederalism. This might make the advance of both substantive demands *and* institutional reforms possible.

Confederation is indeed difficult to imagine. As a result of the historical developments in NSM ideology in the United States, identity politics makes the notion of a shared agenda in this era an elusive idea. Nonetheless, two possibilities exist for intermediate consolidation of social movement interest: institutional reforms that will open up the electoral-representative system, and the promotion of the class ideal as a bridge between disparate identities and issues. Indeed, the two strategies can be combined. It is clear that the efforts of the Greens–USA to forward Ralph Nader in the 2000 presidential race is a promising effort of the type I am describing.

Not surprisingly, Frances Fox Piven and Richard Cloward were instrumental in shaping perhaps the most significant legislative reform to the electoral-representative system in decades—namely the Motor Voter program. By having Congress sponsor voter registration in state-run motor vehicle and welfare agencies, the Motor Voter initiative is one step toward opening up the political process to the institutional influence of nonregistered voters. This can be interpreted as increasing the influence of both the poor and the inchoate social movement sentiment. Similar opportunities hang in the balance with issues like campaign finance reform and other electoral reforms aiming to de-emphasize the bias of a winner-take-all system. In this regard, the agitation for this type of reform could serve as a beginning step in consolidating the interests of fragmented and ideologically inchoate social movement formations and lead, perhaps, to the shaping of a shared identity and agenda.

Institutional reform, it is warned by organizers of various camps, is not a "sexy" issue. But this only underscores the increasingly symbolic quality of both American culture generally and, by association, NSM ideology in the United States. Strategic possibilities such as this continue to be eclipsed by the stubborn attachment to symbolic and identity politics that, in the end, do little to advance or secure the demands of disparate social movements. The lack of NSM reflexivity about the institutional context contributes to missed opportunities.

Institutional reform can be combined most effectively by social movements ideologically committed to a class ideal. It might concretely manifest in a coalition around, for example, universal health care. Health care continues to have enormous appeal among disparate constituencies— ecologists, women's rights advocates, the lesbian and gay community, the working poor, the handicapped, and also those groups disproportionately ranked among the poor including African Americans and Latino Americans (as well as women of all ethnicities). But of course what is clear in such a position is how tentative such a strategy is in the context of American social movements. Resistance to coalition, class-oriented ideologies, and state-related strategies makes generating support for such a combination difficult to achieve.

Social movements today, aimed as they are at securing equality, autonomy, and identity, must indeed begin to become more conscious of their position in their respective national contexts and the international economy. Most importantly, NSM participants need to become increasingly aware of the consequences of withdrawing from the state into what Ulrich Beck calls sub-politics. By abandoning traditional forms of political representation, it is of considerable concern how controls on multinational forces will be developed and applied.

It must be acknowledged that, at least in the United States, there exists a model for such efforts, first in the Poor People's Movement as an extension of the radical vision of the Civil Rights movements, and then again under the Rainbow Coalition until its demise. Indeed, the Rainbow Coalition, comprised as it was of a genuine new social movement base while clearly articulating a class ethic, was a promising experiment that also testifies to the powerful lure and pressures of politics as usual.[13] The lessons and cautions of that experiment are in many respects the starting place for any future efforts aiming for the refocusing of the potential of NSMs in America.

NSMs have indeed afforded a flagging U.S. Left a focus for experimentation and study, both in theory and practice. They have been responsible for articulating the interests of feminism, racial justice, gay and lesbian rights, ecology, youth rights, and peace among others, which often have been overwhelmed by traditional Left approaches. The specific constellation of characteristics that have provoked analysis have offered theorists and activists alike opportunities for reconceptualizing the struggle for social justice and the groundwork for a more just democratic order. Nonetheless, it is difficult to demonstrate that new social movements and their theorists have presented a coherent theoretical alternative to the dominant order. The argument presented throughout this book suggests that the problems evident in new social movements, when considered in the American institutional context, demand a more coherent understanding of the relationship between systemic and contingent process in relation to social, environmental, and political crises. This understanding, I have argued, is the potential province of the radical social movements that remain committed to reflexivity, democracy, and action. At the century's beginning, we have little else upon which to rely.

NOTES

1. Stephen Eric Bronner, *Socialism Unbound* (New York: Routledge, 1990), pp. 167–168.
2. Ibid., p. 166.
3. Ibid., p. 168.
4. Charles Tilly, "Social Movements and National Politics" in *State-Making and Social Movements: Essays in History and Theory*, edited by C. Bright and S. Harding (Ann Arbor: University of Michigan Press, 1988), p. 306.
5. Tilly, "Social Movements, Old and New" in *Research in Social Movements, Conflicts, and Change*, vol. 10 (Greenwich, Conn.: JAI Press, 1988), p. 2.
6. Frances Fox Piven and Richard Cloward, *Poor People's Movements: Why They Succeed, How They Fail* (New York: Vintage Book, 1977), p.11.
7. Ibid., p. 15.
8. Ibid., p. 16.
9. Ibid., p. 17.
10. Ibid., p. ix–x.
11. Ibid.
12. See my discussion in chapter 3 of the restraints of the American political system on social movements.
13. See Sheila Collins, *The Rainbow Challenge: The Jackson Campaign and the Future of U.S. Politics* (New York: Monthly Review Press, 1987), and Manning Marable, "The End of the Rainbow," from *Beyond Black and White* (New York: Verso, 1995).

Bibliography

Bagguley, Paul. "Social Change, the Middle Class and the Emergence of 'New Social Movements': A Critical Analysis." *Sociological Review*, vol. 40 (1992).

Barber, Benjamin. *Jihad Versus McWorld*. New York: Ballantine, 1996.

Barker, Ernest. *Principles of Social and Political Theory*. London: Oxford University Press, 1961.

Beard, Charles. *The Economic Basis of Politics and Related Writings*. New York: Vintage, 1975.

Beck, Ulrich. *The Risk Society: Towards a New Modernity*. London: Sage, 1992.

Boggs, Carl. *Social Movements and Political Power*. Philadelphia: Temple University Press, 1986.

Boisvert, Raymond. *Dewey's Metaphysics*. New York: Fordham University Press, 1988.

Braun, Aurel, and Stephen Scheinberg. *The Extreme Right: Freedom and Security at Risk*. New York: Westview, 1997.

Bronner, Stephen Eric. *Of Critical Theory and Its Theorists*. Cambridge: Blackwell, 1994.

———. *Moments of Decision*. New York: Routledge, 1989.

———. *Socialism Unbound*. New York: Routledge, 1990.

Carnoy, Martin, and Henry M. Levin. *The Limits of Education Reform*. New York: Longman, 1976.

Carnoy, Martin. *The State and Political Theory*. Princeton, N.J.: Princeton University Press, 1984.

Cassell, Philip, ed. *The Giddens Reader*. Stanford, Calif.: Stanford University Press, 1993.

Cohen, Jean. *Class and Civil Society: The Limits of Marxian Critical Theory*. London: Oxford, 1982.

———. "Strategy or Identity: New Theoretical Paradigms and Contemporary Social Movements." *Social Research*, vol. 52, no. 4 (Winter 1985).

Collins, Sheila. *The Rainbow Challenge: The Jackson Campaign and the Future of U.S. Politics.* New York: Monthly Review, 1987.

Cotgrove, S., and A. Duff. "Environmentalism, Values and Social Change." *Sociological Review,* vol. 28, no. 2 (1981).

Croll, Elizabeth. *Feminism and Socialism in China.* New York: Schocken, 1980.

Darnovsky, M., Barbara Epstein, and Richard Flacks, eds. *Cultural Politics and Social Movements.* Philadelphia: Temple University Press, 1995.

Davis, Mike. *Prisoners of the American Dream.* London: Verso, 1986.

Dewey, John. *Characters and Events: Popular Essays in Social and Political Philosophy.* Edited by Joseph Ratner. New York: Henry Holt, 1929.

———. *Logic: The Theory of Inquiry.* New York: Henry Holt, 1938.

———. *The Public and Its Problems.* Athens, Ohio: Swallow Press/Ohio University Press, 1991.

———. *The Quest for Certainty: A Study of the Relation of Knowledge and Action.* New York: Putnam, 1960.

Diamond, Sarah. *Roads to Dominion: Right Wing Movements and Political Power in the United States.* New York: Guilford, 1995.

Diani, Mario. "The Concept of Social Movement." *Sociological Review,* vol. 40 (1992).

Dicker, Georges. *Dewey's Theory of Knowing.* Philadelphia: University City Science Center, 1976.

Diggins, John Patrick. "Acknowledge and Sorrow: Louis Hartz's Quarrel with American History." *Political Theory,* vol. 16, no. 3 (August 1988).

Duyvendak, Jan Williem. *The Power of Politics: New Social Movements in France.* Boulder, Colo.: Westview, 1995.

Echols, Alice. *Daring to Be Bad: Radical Feminism in America, 1967–75.* Minneapolis: University of Minnesota Press, 1989.

Elliot, J. ed. *The Debate of the State Conventions on the Adoption of the Federal Constitution, As Recommended by the General Convention at Philadelphia in 1787.* Philadelphia, 1866.

Ellis, Joseph. *American Sphinx: The Character of Thomas Jefferson.* New York: Knopf, 1997.

Eyerman, Ron. "Social Movements and Social Theory." *Sociology,* vol. 18 (February 1984).

Farber, David. *Chicago '68.* Chicago: University of Chicago Press, 1988.

Fine, Nathan. *Labor and Farmer Parties in the United States, 1828-1928.* New York: Rand School of Social Science, 1928.

Foucault, Michel. *Power/Knowledge.* New York: Pantheon, 1980.

Freeman, Jo. "The Tyranny of Structurelessness." In *Feminist Revolution* [edited by Kathie Sarachild]. New York: Random House, 1975, 1978.

Fukuyama, Frances. "The End of History?" *The National Interest* (Summer 1989).

Garrow, David. *Bearing the Cross: Martin Luther King, Jr., and the Southern Christian Leadership Conference.* New York: Vintage, 1986.

Gitlin, Todd. *The Sixties: Years of Hope, Days of Rage.* New York: Bantam, 1987.
———. *The Whole World Is Watching: Mass Media in the Making and Unmaking of the New Left.* Berkeley: University of California Press, 1980.
Glick, Brian. *Cointelpro.* Boston: South End, 1989.
Goldman, Eric. *A Rendezvous with Destiny: A History of Modern American Reform.* New York: Vintage, 1956, 1977.
Goodwyn, Lawrence. *The Populist Movement.* London: Oxford University Press, 1980.
———. *Democratic Promise.* London: Oxford University Press, 1978.
Habermas, Jurgen. *Between Facts and Norms.* Cambridge, Mass.: MIT Press, 1996.
———. *The New Conservatism: Cultural Criticism and the Historians' Debate.* Cambridge, Mass.: MIT Press, 1992.
———. *Philosophical Discourse of Modernity.* Trans. by Frederick Lawrence. Cambridge, Mass.: MIT Press, 1987.
———. "The Public Sphere: An Encyclopedia Article." Trans. by Sarah Lennox and Frank Lennox. *New German Critique*, vol. 1, no. 3 (1974).
———. *The Structural Transformation of the Public Sphere.* Cambridge, Mass.: MIT Press, 1982.
———. "Tasks of a Critical Social Theory." In *Jurgen Habermas on Society and Politics,* edited by Stephen Seidman. Boston: Beacon, 1989.
———. *The Theory of Communicative Action, Volumes 1 and 2.* Boston: Beacon, 1984.
Hanisch, Carol. "The Liberal Take-Over of the Women's Liberation Movement." In *Feminist Revolution* [edited by Kathie Sarachild]. New York: Random House, 1975, 1978.
———. "What Can Be Learned: A Critique of the Miss America Pageant." In *Voices from Women's Liberation,* edited by Leslie Tanner. New York: New American Library, 1970.
Hannigan, John A. "Alain Touraine, Manuel Castells and Social Movement Theory: A Critical Appraisal." *Sociological Quarterly,* vol. 26 (Winter 1985).
Hartz, Louis. *The Liberal Tradition in America.* New York: Harcourt Brace and World, 1955.
Hobbes, Thomas. *Leviathan.* New York: Viking Penguin, 1985.
Hoffman, Abbie. *Soon to Be a Major Motion Picture.* New York: Putnam, 1980.
Hofstadter, Richard. *The Age of Reform.* New York: Knopf, 1955.
Horkheimer, Max. "The Latest Attack on Metaphysics" and "Traditional and Critical Theory." In *Critical Theory: Selected Essays.* New York: Herder and Herder, 1972.
———. "The State of Contemporary Social Philosophy and the Tasks of an Institute for Social Research." Trans. by Peter Wagner. In *Critical Theory and Society,* edited by Stephen Bronner and Douglas Kellner. New York: Routledge, 1989.

Jenness, Valerie, and Kendal Broad. *Hate Crimes: New Social Movements and the Politics of Violence.* New York: Aldine Greyter, 1997.

Joll, James. *Gramsci.* Glasgow, Scotland: Fontana Collins, 1977.

Kant, Immanuel. *Groundwork of the Metaphysics of Morals.* New York: Harper Torchbooks, 1959.

Katsiafikas, George. *The Imagination of the New Left: A Global Analysis of 1968.* Boston: South End, 1987.

——. *The Subversion of Politics.* Atlantic Highlands, N.J.: Humanities Press, 1997.

Kitchelt, Herbert. *The Radical Right in Western Europe.* Ann Arbor: University of Michigan Press, 1995.

——. "Social Movements, Political Parties and Democratic Theory." *American Academy of Political and Social Science*, vol. 528 (July 1993).

Kivisto, Peter. "Contemporary Social Movements in Advanced Industrial Societies and Sociological Intervention: An Appraisal of Alain Touraine's *Pratique.*" *Acta Sociologica*, vol. 27 (1984).

Klandermans, Bert, and Sydney Tarrow. "Mobilization into Social Movements: Synthesizing European and American Approaches." *International Social Movement Research*, vol. 1 (1988).

Koopmans, Ruud. *Democracy from Below: New Social Movements and the Political System in West Germany.* Boulder, Colo.: Westview, 1995.

Kriesi, Hanspeter, Rudd Koopermans, Jan Williem Duyvendak, and Marco G. Giugni. *New Social Movements in Western Europe: A Comparative Analysis.* London: University College of London Press, 1995.

Laclau, Ernesto. *New Reflections on the Revolution of Our Time.* London: Verso, 1990.

Laclau, Ernesto, and Chantal Mouffe. *Hegemony and Socialist Strategy.* London: Verso, 1985.

Landes, Joan. *Women and the Public Sphere in the Age of the French Revolution.* Ithaca, N.Y.: Cornell University Press, 1988.

Larana, Enrique, Hank Johnston, and Joseph R. Gusfield, eds. *New Social Movements: From Ideology to Identity.* Philadelphia: Temple University Press, 1994.

Lipset, Seymour Martin, and John H. M. Laslett. *Failure of a Dream?* Berkeley: University of California Press, 1974, 1984.

Lowi, Theodore. *The End of Liberalism: The Second Republic of the United States.* New York: W. W. Norton, 1979, 1969.

MacPherson, Crawford Brough. *The Political Theory of Possessive Individualism: Hobbes to Locke.* Oxford: Oxford University Press, 1962, 1990.

Madison, James. "No. 10." In *The Federalist Papers*, edited by Isaac Kramnick. London: Penguin Books, 1987.

Marable, Manning. *Beyond Black and White: Transforming African-American Politics.* New York: Verso, 1995.

Marcuse, Herbert. *One Dimensional Man: Studies in the Ideology of Advanced Industrial Society.* Boston: Beacon, 1964.

McAdam, Doug. *Freedom Summer.* New York: Oxford University Press, 1988.

———. *Political Process and the Development of Black Insurgency, 1930–70.* Chicago: University of Chicago Press, 1982.

McAdam, Doug, and Dieter Rucht. "The Cross-National Diffusion of Movement Ideas." *Annals of the Academy of Political and Social Science*, vol. 528 (July 1993).

McCarthy, John, and Mayer Zald. "Resource Mobilization and Social Movements: A Partial Theory." *American Journal of Sociology*, vol. 82, no. 6 (1977).

McCormick, Richard P. "The Party Period and Public Policy: An Exploratory Hypothesis." *Journal of American History*, vol. 66 (September 1979).

———. *From Realignment to Reform: Political Change in New York State, 1893-1910.* Ithaca, N.Y.: Cornell University Press, 1981.

Melucci, Alberto. *Nomads of the Present.* Philadelphia: Temple University Press, 1989.

———. "The Symbolic Challenge of Contemporary Movements." *Social Research*, vol. 52, no. 4 (Winter 1985).

Miller, James. *Democracy Is in the Streets.* New York: Simon and Schuster, 1987.

Mills, Amy Chen. *CIA Off Campus: Building the Movement against Agency Recruitment and Research.* Boston, Mass.: South End, 1991.

Morris, Aldon, and Carol McClurg Mueller, eds. *Frontiers in Social Movement Theory.* New Haven, Conn.: Yale University Press, 1991.

Mouffe, Chantal, ed. *Gramsci and Marxist Theory.* London: Routledge, 1979.

Neal, Patrick. "In the Shadow of the General Will: Rawls, Kant, and Rousseau on the Problem of Political Right." *Review of Politics* (1988).

Offe, Claus. *Contradictions of the Welfare State.* London: Hutchinson, 1984.

———. "New Social Movements: Challenging the Boundaries of Institutional Politics." *Social Research*, vol. 52, no. 4 (Winter 1985).

———. "Democracy against the Welfare State? Structural Foundations of Neo-conservative Political Opportunities." *Political Theory*, vol. 15 (November 1987).

Oloffson, Gunnar. "After the Working-Class Movement? An Essay on What's 'New' and What's 'Social' in the New Social Movements." *Acta Sociologica*, vol. 31 (1988).

Olson, Mancur. *The Logic of Collective Action: Public Goods and the Theory of Groups.* Cambridge: Harvard University Press, 1968.

Pearlman, Selig. *A Theory of the Labor Movement.* New York: Macmillan, 1928.

Piven, Frances Fox, and Richard Cloward. *Poor People's Movements: How They Succeed, Why They Fail.* New York: Vintage, 1977, 1979.

———. *Regulating the Poor: The Functions of Public Welfare.* New York: Vintage, 1971, 1993.

———. *Why Americans Don't Vote: Turnout Decline in the United States, 1960–1984.* New York: Pantheon, 1988.

Rhoads, Robert A. *Freedom's Web: Student Activism in an Age of Cultural Diversity.* Baltimore, Md.: Johns Hopkins University Press, 1998.

Rorty, Richard. *Consequences of Pragmatism: Essays, 1972–1980.* Minneapolis: University of Minnesota Press, 1982.

Rustin, Michael. "Incomplete Modernity: Ulrich Beck's *Risk Society.*" *Dissent* (Summer 1994).

Sale, Kirkpatrick. *SDS: Ten Years toward a Revolution.* New York: Random House, 1973.

Saloutos, Theodore A. "Radicalism and the Agrarian Tradition." In *Failure of a Dream? Essays in the History of American Socialism,* edited by John H. M. Laslett and Seymour M. Lipset. Berkeley: University of California Press, 1984.

Schattschneider, E. E. *The Semisovereign People.* New York: Holt, Reinhart and Winston, 1960.

Schlozman, Kay, and John T. Tierney. *Organized Interest and American Democracy.* New York: Harper and Row, 1985.

Scott, Alan. "Action, Movement, and Intervention: Reflections on the Sociology of Alan Touraine." *Canadian Review of Sociology and Anthropology,* vol. 28 (1991).

———. *Ideology and the New Social Movements.* London: Unwin Hyman, 1990.

Sennett, Richard. *The Fall of Public Man.* New York: Vantage, 1976.

Sombart, Werner. *Why Is There No Socialism in America?* Edited by C. T. Husbands. White Plains, N.Y.: M. E. Sharpe, 1976.

Stern, Kenneth. *A Force upon the Plain: The American Militia Movement and the Politics of Hate.* New York: Simon and Schuster, 1996.

Tilly, Charles. *The Contentious French.* Cambridge: Belknap, 1986.

———. *From Mobilization to Revolution.* Englewood Cliffs, N.J.: Prentice Hall, 1978.

———. "Models and Realities of Popular Collective Action." *Social Research,* vol. 52, no. 4 (1985).

———. "Social Movements and National Politics." In *State-Making and Social Movements: Essays in History and Theory,* edited by C. Bright and S. Harding. Ann Arbor: University of Michigan Press, 1988.

———. "Social Movements, Old and New." In *Research in Social Movements, Conflicts, and Change,* vol. 10. Greenwich, Conn.: JAI Press, 1988.

Tilly, Charles, Louise Tilly, and Richard Tilly. *The Rebellious Century: 1830–1930.* Cambridge, Mass.: Harvard University Press, 1977.

Touraine, Alain. *Critique of Modernity.* Cambridge, Mass.: Blackwell, 1995.

———. "An Introduction to the Study of Social Movements." *Social Research,* vol. 52, no. 4 (Winter 1985).

Tucker, Kenneth. "Ideology and Social Movements: The Contributions of Habermas." *Sociological Inquiry,* vol. 59, no.1 (February 1989).

Turner, Ralph, and Lewis Killian.*Collective Behavior.* 3d ed. Englewood Cliffs, N.J.: Prentice Hall, 1986.

Vellela, Tony. *New Voices: Student Political Activism in the '80's and '90's.* Boston: South End, 1988.

Weinstein, James. *The Corporate Ideal in the Liberal State: 1900–1918.* Boston: Beacon, 1969).

Zinn, Howard. *A People's History of the United States.* New York: Harper Collins, 1980.

Index

About the Author

Christine Kelly was a student activist in the 1980s and 1990s. She earned her Ph.D. in political theory at Rutgers University in 1996. She was a visiting assistant professor at Mount Holyoke College for three years and is currently assistant professor of political science and women's studies at the University of Northern Colorado. Dr. Kelly's articles have appeared in *Peace Review, New Political Science*, and political journals in France and Italy. She received the 1999 Christian Bay Award for Best Section Paper, presented by the Caucus for New Political Science of the American Political Science Association.